How to Set Boundaries

Master the Art of Saying No, Stop People-Pleasing, and Command Respect without Feeling Guilty

© Copyright 2023 - All rights reserved.

The content contained within this book may not be reproduced, duplicated, or transmitted without direct written permission from the author or the publisher.

Under no circumstances will any blame or legal responsibility be held against the publisher, or author, for any damages, reparation, or monetary loss due to the information contained within this book, either directly or indirectly.

Legal Notice:

This book is copyright protected. It is only for personal use. You cannot amend, distribute, sell, use, quote or paraphrase any part, or the content within this book, without the consent of the author or publisher.

Disclaimer Notice:

Please note the information contained within this document is for educational and entertainment purposes only. All effort has been executed to present accurate, up-to-date, reliable, and complete information. No warranties of any kind are declared or implied. Readers acknowledge that the author is not engaging in the rendering of legal, financial, medical, or professional advice. The content within this book has been derived from various sources. Please consult a licensed professional before attempting any techniques outlined in this book.

By reading this document, the reader agrees that under no circumstances is the author responsible for any losses, direct or indirect, that are incurred as a result of the use of the information contained within this document, including, but not limited to, errors, omissions, or inaccuracies.

Free Bonus from Andy Gardner

Hi!

My name is Andy Gardner, and first off, I want to THANK YOU for reading my book.

Now you have a chance to join my exclusive email list related to human psychology and self-development so you can get the ebook below for free as well as the potential to get more ebooks for free! Simply click the link below to join.

P.S. Remember that it's 100% free to join the list.

Access your free bonuses here:
https://livetolearn.lpages.co/andy-gardner-how-to-set-boundaries-paperback/

Table of Contents

INTRODUCTION 1
CHAPTER 1: THE BENEFITS OF SETTING BOUNDARIES 3
CHAPTER 2: HOW TO AVOID GUILT AND SET HEALTHY BOUNDARIES 11
CHAPTER 3: HOW TO TURN INSECURITY INTO CONFIDENCE 24
CHAPTER 4: 6 MISTAKES THAT RUIN YOUR LOVE LIFE 34
CHAPTER 5: TEN EFFECTIVE WAYS TO DEAL WITH DIFFICULT FAMILY MEMBERS 45
CHAPTER 6: HOW TO IMMEDIATELY IMPROVE YOUR CHILD'S BEHAVIOR 55
CHAPTER 7: 7 PSYCHOLOGICAL TRICKS TO DEAL WITH NEGATIVE FRIENDS 65
CHAPTER 8: HOW TO GET THAT PROMOTION WITHOUT PEOPLE PLEASING 75
CHAPTER 9: 10 MISTAKES THAT MAY MAKE YOU SEEM FAKE 84
CHAPTER 10: HOW TO MAKE YOUR BOUNDARIES 10X MORE EFFECTIVE 93
CONCLUSION 104
HERE'S ANOTHER BOOK BY ANDY GARDNER THAT YOU MIGHT LIKE 106
FREE BONUS FROM ANDY GARDNER 107
REFERENCES 108

Introduction

Take a trip down memory lane and think about the time you spent in elementary school geography lessons. Do you remember your instructor pulling out a world map and explaining how different colored lines denoted national borders?

A physical feature, such as a river, can sometimes serve as a natural boundary between territories, but in most cases, the markings we see on the map do not exist in the real world. Although we can't see them, we know when we've become too close to another country's territory, and we back off.

For various reasons, this concept is much easier to grasp on a map than in our relationships. Unfortunately, we seldom encounter situations in which we are separated from others by actual physical walls. Even though there are limits, these barriers may not always work, and other individuals may breach the line in some way.

This is when establishing some emotional or psychological distance comes into play. That is how you communicate your limits to others in terms of things like moral support and physical labor, asking for help or guidance, and how frequently you're expected to check in with them.

Despite the prevalence of discussions on the need to maintain healthy emotional and personal boundaries, doing so can be easier said than done. We've heard that we should "establish limits," but what does that mean, and how do we do it?

This isn't a topic we covered in class like geography. There has never been widespread instruction on how to use it to promote good connections in our personal lives, so most of us need to learn how through our personal experience.

This book contains a step-by-step guide to setting boundaries, which can help you keep good professional, personal, and social relationships, all while protecting your mental, social, and emotional health. Compared to other resources, this book is more accessible and user-friendly and takes a practical, hands-on approach.

Do you ever fantasize about how different your life could be if the people who matter most to you honored your need for space?

How often do you wish there was a simple method to avoid saying "Yes" when you don't feel like it?

Do you wish to explore self-love without feeling guilty?

If this sounds like you, you have probably spent too much time making other people happy.

Perhaps you always say "Yes" out of fear that the other person will be disappointed or angry if you say "No," forcing you to do things you never wanted to do in the first place.

If it occurs too often, people may soon begin to take you for granted and expect you to do things you do not want to do. Your use of the word "No" slips further and further away. Others may describe you as harsh or gloomy if you attempt to establish limits. Getting other people to appreciate your judgments and needs without causing disagreement may also seem difficult.

This book will teach you how to take care of yourself and set limits without feeling bad or guilty.

The road ahead may be rocky, demanding introspection into your motivations and thought processes, but with these adjustments, you will be able to set firm boundaries and stick to them when they are tested.

As well as this, you'll discover methods to overcome the fear that comes with setting boundaries and the guilt that comes with the potential of distancing loved ones.

I hope you use this opportunity to learn about yourself and revel in your successes.

Chapter 1: The Benefits of Setting Boundaries

People-pleasing is a game that almost everyone plays, to one degree or another. It's easy to get caught up in pleasing other people with our words, actions, and decisions. However, doing so at the expense of your personal wellbeing is not healthy. In fact, consistently putting the needs of others before your own can have negative effects on your mental health and can lead to feelings of resentment, stress, and anxiety. Without knowing and establishing boundaries, attempting to please everybody can be draining. It'll take your time, energy, and mental and emotional space. There are many ways that people can be toxic or negative in our lives, whether it's a friend who drains you by constantly asking for favors without reciprocating, a family member who is consistently negative and brings you down, or a partner who manipulates and controls you.

There's a fine line between people-pleasing and setting healthy boundaries.
https://www.pexels.com/photo/photo-of-men-having-conversation-935949/

In any of these scenarios and others not yet mentioned, it's crucial that you understand the benefits of setting boundaries with other people so that you don't continue to give them something (in this case, your time, energy, etc.) that they won't give back. This chapter will explore why and how setting boundaries with others is a healthy way to protect yourself from being taken advantage of.

What Are Personal Boundaries?

Boundaries represent a fundamental pillar for healthy self-esteem and healthy relationships alike. "Boundaries as a Recovery Concept," written by Peggy L. Ferguson, Ph.D., highlights how the ability to set healthy boundaries also signals that a recovering addict or trauma victim is improving. Therefore, bringing boundaries forward clearly signifies good social integration or reintegration. Boundaries are the invisible walls that keep you safe from people and things outside your comfort zone. They're the lines you draw to keep people, ideas, activities, or situations at a distance. The key to staying healthy and happy is establishing boundaries for yourself. Boundaries help protect you from stress, anxiety, and burnout. If you don't have clear boundaries in your life, it can be difficult to know when it's time to say "No" to something new or tempting. When you establish boundaries for yourself, it helps you feel more in control of your life. You'll know when to step away from situations that are too much for you to handle when they arrive. Boundaries also help prevent burnout by giving you the space and time to recharge when needed.

As we grow up, we learn to recognize the people in our lives. We develop a sense of who is "us" versus who is "them." The ability to recognize ourselves as separate from others is one of the most significant developmental milestones we can achieve. Being able to differentiate between "us" and "them" allows us to develop boundaries between ourselves and others (and not feel like we need to merge with them!). As children, we want to belong and want to be accepted. We want people to like us, trust us, and see us as an extension of ourselves. If this doesn't happen, we tend to become very clingy or overly dependent on other people in order to feel safe, secure, and validated. To understand your boundaries or lack of boundaries, you need to look at the physical, emotional, and cognitive factors that influence them. Once you know more about these underlying factors, you can start to understand what triggers your lack of boundaries and how to respond in a way that feels appropriate for you. Here are some boundaries you should consider to help you to maintain your sense of self.

Physical Boundaries

Boundaries are an essential part of any interrelationship. While they can feel like an added inconvenience or a restriction at first, once you get used to them, they can help keep your relationships healthy and prevent over-involvement. Physical boundaries can help protect people from uncomfortable or unsafe situations, as well as help prevent forms of emotional or physical abuse. They can also help other people respect your time by preventing them from interrupting you while you're talking with someone or doing something else.

To set physical boundaries effectively, you need to know yourself and what feels comfortable and safe for you. You may have different boundaries for your personal life than for your work life, for example. It is also essential to communicate your boundaries clearly and honestly so that your partner and the people around you understand what is expected of them and why. Physical boundary setting doesn't have to be confrontational or argumentative. It can be as simple as saying "No" or "Stop" when you need space or sitting down with your partner, colleague, friend, or family member when you want to talk about something that makes you feel uncomfortable. Be clear about what you want. The key is to state your values upfront so that everyone is on the same page from the beginning. Knowing what you value most will help you to determine whether someone is a good match for you, and it will help you to know when you're being over-involved in a relationship (or under-involved). Furthermore, physical boundary setting should never be used as a way to control your partner. It should be a mutual decision between the two of you. Keep in mind that boundaries are not set in stone. They can change over time if they no longer feel appropriate for the situation at hand.

Emotional Boundaries

Boundaries are an essential tool in establishing emotional health. They help us to set clear and healthy limits on how we interact with others and ourselves. When we don't have strong boundaries, we may feel powerless and unable to control our feelings or behavior. For example, someone who is in a toxic relationship may struggle to leave the situation because they feel like they can't trust themselves or their own judgment. On the other hand, someone who has healthy boundaries can comfortably end a relationship without feeling overwhelmed by sadness or regret. To establish healthy boundaries, make sure you are specific about what you want and need from others. Clearly set out your expectations so you can avoid feeling disappointed or hurt when those expectations aren't met. At the same time, being clear about your needs can help you to take care of yourself when you need space or support.

Sexual Boundaries

First and foremost, it is crucial that you recognize which events make you feel violated. This means that there are signs that your boundaries are being crossed. If your partner is constantly trying to make you have sex with them, or if they constantly want to touch you in ways that make you feel uncomfortable, then this is an indication that they are violating your boundaries. These signs can be subtle, so be sure to listen carefully to what your partner is saying. If they say that they love you, but you feel uncomfortable with them touching you in certain ways, then these are signs that they are violating your boundaries. If the other person consistently ignores the situation or tries to justify their actions by saying things like "It's not a big deal" or "It's just a hug," then these are also indicators that they are violating your boundaries.

The first step in establishing sexual boundaries with other people is knowing when you are being violated. Once this is established, the next step is to clearly communicate these feelings to the other person. This can be done in a variety of ways by openly stating how you feel (e.g., "I don't want to have sex with you right now"), by explicitly asking for what you want (e.g., "Can we please stop?"), and by being open and direct about what you want from your sexual relationship (e.g., "I like it/don't like it when...")

Intellectual Boundaries

Intellectual boundaries are a guide to how far you allow others to get into your head. These boundaries help keep the peace and can be established by you or others. They can also be negotiated and set by you if you suspect that someone is trying to control you. When someone insults your beliefs, they are sharing an opinion that is completely inappropriate and unsupportive of you. Insulting someone's beliefs means dismissing them as wrong, silly, or immature. Crossing these barriers can happen in many different ways. It can be passive-aggressive and mean-spirited, like when someone tells you you're being too sensitive or that you shouldn't be so emotional. It can also be more direct and active when someone says something directly to you, like, "You know what? I really don't think that you should care about the environment at all! You should get in your car and go for a drive!" A common form of someone crossing intellectual boundaries is to belittle someone by saying that their way of thinking is "Just a phase," or "You'll grow out of it soon," or "You're new to this – you don't know what you're talking about!"

The fact that intellectual boundaries exist is a good thing because they protect our sense of self from being molded by others. We are strong when we are true to our personal values and beliefs. But when someone tries to diminish what we believe in, then we need to establish more intellectual boundaries.

Financial Boundaries

Setting a financial boundary for each person in your relationship allows both partners some financial autonomy. This way, one partner doesn't have to worry about spending more than the other and can enjoy their own finances without feeling guilty. Money in relationships can be tricky. It's easy for both parties to feel like their partner is pulling the short straw or keeping them from having a good time. Money issues can cause tension and stress and even lead to arguments.

To make money work in your relationship, there are some things you should keep in mind:

1. **Know your partner's financial situation.** This will give you a better idea of how much money they have and what they can afford.
2. **Discuss how you want to spend money and what it means to each of you.** Let them know how their spending affects your life and your finances, so they understand how their decisions affect you.
3. **If you have joint accounts, make sure both of you have access to them.** If one person doesn't have access to the account, that person needs to get permission from the other before making any changes to the account, which can feel restrictive.
4. **Talk about what each person is responsible for when it comes to paying bills, paying rent or mortgage payments, and buying groceries.** Make sure each person understands their responsibilities, so there aren't any surprises later on.

5. **If one person pays more than the other, try and split it 50/50** or at least make sure both people understand where their money is going so there aren't any surprises, upsets, or passive-aggressive hard feelings.

Benefits of Setting Boundaries

Setting boundaries helps you identify your personal limits and assert your needs and wants. It gives you the power to say no when you need to, to express your desires and feelings, and to have a sense of control over your life. Setting boundaries also allows you to prioritize your time, energy, and attention, which can be very empowering. They benefit not only you but also those around you. For example, family members are more likely to respect and honor your wishes if they know where they stand with you. They will also feel less anxious when they know what's expected of them. Friends are more likely to be considerate of your time if they know how much time you have available for them. As a result, everyone benefits from clear, defined boundaries. But to do this, you need to overcome your fear of saying "No" and embrace assertiveness.

You'll Be a Better Communicator

When two people don't agree on boundaries, there are often misunderstandings and arguments that take place. Without communicating your needs, you'll be stuck in a perpetual cycle of drama, feeling victimized, misunderstood, and disrespected – all while trying to establish boundaries. Essentially, they are not possible without vocalizing what it is you want. Knowing where the other person stands on boundaries helps you respect them and communicate effectively. Having clear boundaries will allow you to feel safe and secure and express yourself clearly. By communicating your needs and setting clear boundaries, you are more likely to get what you want out of a relationship and in your professional life.

You'll Become More Assertive

There is no shortage of reasons why people struggle to set boundaries. Some people struggle because they have a hard time saying "No." Maybe you are afraid of hurting someone's feelings or making them angry. Maybe you are worried that you'll look bad if you stand up for yourself. Or you could just be misinterpreting other people's signals. With so many reasons to struggle, it's no wonder setting boundaries can be a difficult task. So, how can you overcome these obstacles?

First and foremost, you need to acknowledge that other people's opinions of you and your boundaries should never dictate how or when you set them. Then, identify the reasons why you struggle with setting them in the first place. Once you know what's holding you back, you can start to overcome them one by one. For example, if you tend to get defensive when someone questions your decision-making process, then you could try practicing being more assertive until those negative emotions are replaced with more positive ones like confidence and self-awareness.

You'll Develop Independence

Boundaries are the lines that you draw around the things you are willing to do. When it comes to independence, setting boundaries is an essential first step toward knowing what you are and are not willing to do. For example, if you can't stay late at work (because you're looking forward to your favorite takeout food after a long and busy week), then put your foot down by making yourself a priority. Another aspect of independence is the ability to make decisions for yourself.

You'll Create a Sense of Peace and Safety

If you do not have clear boundaries with yourself, you'll feel like an outsider who does not belong in your own life. If you have clear boundaries with yourself and others, you'll be more likely to feel safe and at peace with yourself and other people. Having strong boundaries also makes you more compassionate. It helps you be more empathetic and more understanding of other people's needs and feelings. When you're able to recognize the need for autonomy, it can also result in a sense of self-reliance, which contributes to emotional resilience.

You'll Take a Proactive Approach to Future Conflicts

Setting boundaries is the best thing you can do to prevent future conflicts from happening. Boundaries are lines that define what you and the people in your life should and should not do. If everyone at work and those within your inner circle has different ideas about what is acceptable, or if one of you feels left out or uncertain about something, it will be very difficult to make any progress. Boundaries help you to set clear rules that everyone can follow so that everyone knows what is expected of them. They also help you to feel more confident in your decisions and more in control of your life. By establishing boundaries, you take a step away from blaming and taking responsibility for everything that happens in your relationship. You are no longer responsible for making sure that everything goes perfectly for both of you. Instead, you can focus on understanding each other better and learning how to deal with the ups and downs of life together.

You'll Be Putting Yourself First

By setting clear and reasonable limits, you can ensure that your needs are being met.

They're about examining how much support, time, and energy you're willing to give someone else. If you're not capable of giving them what they are asking of you, then don't give it to them. The more you do, the more likely you are to get frustrated and burnt out. By setting boundaries, you can feel more in control of your life and will be able to experience less stress as a result. You're saying "no" to things that are causing you stress. Once you've said "no" to these things, it will be easier for you to say "yes" to other things that are more important to you. You'll also find that others will respect your boundaries and are likely to choose other options that are more aligned with your values.

In life, there are many people who are willing to give you their time for free. These people can be friends, family members, neighbors, or even acquaintances that you meet online. However, when it comes to interacting with them on a personal level, you need to set boundaries so that you do not become overextended and resent them later. Setting boundaries is not something that many people consider doing unless they have been taken advantage of by someone else repeatedly. However, setting boundaries can make your life easier while also protecting your time and energy as a resource in your life.

Knowing the benefits of setting boundaries will provide you with the incentive to establish them. Now that you have a better idea of what needs to be done, continue reading to discover a wealth of information and actionable steps you can take to learn this essential life skill.

Chapter 2: How to Avoid Guilt and Set Healthy Boundaries

Boundaries are the restrictions that you establish in your relationships. They set your limits for what is permitted and prohibited. Setting and sticking to limits is crucial to our mental and emotional health. Inappropriate feelings of guilt could lead to tension that prevents us from expressing our disapproval of something to others. If you feel bad about establishing a boundary, you have some limiting beliefs in your head.

In this chapter, we'll talk about the difference between healthy and unhealthy forms of guilt and how to reframe negative thoughts and processes for imposing boundaries and letting go of guilt.

It's important to set healthy boundaries to avoid unjustified feelings of guilt.
https://www.pexels.com/photo/multiracial-friends-bullying-female-on-street-6147385/

Boundaries are important for self-care because they act as a safeguard against harm when they are established. It is crucial for your health and mental wellbeing to set, keep, and enforce limits beyond what you want for yourself.

Adaptive and Maladaptive Guilt: Are You Guilty or Not?

Adaptive guilt is helpful since it encourages us to improve. When we act in a way that goes against our values, we naturally feel guilty. In contrast, the twisted perspective that leads to maladaptive guilt may stem from cultural beliefs, religious teachings, early life events, or excessive self-criticism.

Adaptive Guilt

So, your moral code dictates that you should not intentionally harm others. For example, it's natural and healthy to feel guilty when your careless driving causes physical harm to another person. You feel bad about what you did and want to make amends.

Adaptive guilt motivates you to change your ways and uphold your values.

Maladaptive Guilt

Maladaptive guilt is frequently caused by religious or cultural teachings or overly critical evaluations of one's character and behavior. Maladaptive guilt undermines your sense of self and wellbeing and makes you feel uneasy. Maladaptive guilt is tilted toward unfavorable concepts.

It's Time to Restructure

When you look at yourself through a critical lens, it's easy to be harsh on yourself and feel as if you've been selfish, inconsiderate, impolite, or otherwise unpleasant. If you engage in self-critical, negative self-talk that leads to maladaptive guilt, failure is unavoidable. Restructuring, in this case, would imply arguing against the negative idea with a true statement about yourself.

Rather than ruminating on your supposed lack of friendliness, try repeating the following claims to yourself and thinking about how they relate to you.

"I have the right to privacy."

"I am a reliable companion."

"Great friends may communicate freely and honestly with one another."

"If I tell her something and politely ask her not to tell anyone else, it doesn't make me less of a friend."

Addressing negative thoughts by focusing on the facts may help you to move forward in a more positive direction.

Boundaries: Healthy vs. Unhealthy

Many individuals struggle to establish and maintain healthy limits. You may not even know what healthy limits are if you have trouble saying "No" or standing up for yourself. If you were raised without appropriate boundaries, you might need to learn some.

Healthy Boundary

Any restriction that helps you feel safe and secure is a healthy boundary. It's a chance to specify your limits and choose what actions to accept or reject.

When you establish healthy boundaries, you can also make sure there are repercussions for crossing them. These consequences may seem harsh or pointless, but they will help you show how seriously you take your rules.

If your spouse crosses an emotional or physical line, you may choose to confront them about it and express your worries.

Some examples of healthy limits include the following:

- Being aware of yourself and the ability to express your needs and desires effectively to others
- Respecting your boundaries and not sacrificing them for the sake of others
- Refusing to give in and handling rejection well
- Retaining your sense of identity and refusing to allow others to shape your worth by other people's opinions
- Recognizing that your emotions are valid and your needs are worthy of respect and consideration

- Being considerate of other people's viewpoints without lowering your standards or compromising your morals

Unhealthy Boundaries

Unhealthy boundaries are those that need to be clarified or enforced more consistently. You may try to set a limit but need help sticking to it or talking to people about it when problems arise. Many people lack personal boundaries in their relationships, which can result in domineering or dependent behavior.

Unhealthy limits also include any restrictions or limitations you use to exert control over your relationships with family and friends. Keep in mind that your boundaries exist to help you, not to control others.

Relationships with unhealthy boundaries can display a disturbing trend of disrespect. When one person has trouble setting and sticking to limits, the other may find it difficult to respect them.

These acts may lead to toxic behaviors, including domineering conduct, invasion of privacy, and a lack of respect for personal space. For relationships with other people to work, both sides must agree to set and stick to reasonable limits.

The following are some examples of unhealthy boundaries:
- Acting disrespectfully toward another person because you disagree with their principles, beliefs, or viewpoints
- Not being able to accept rejection or say "No" to others
- Taking up the burden of caring for the emotions and wellbeing of others
- A sense that it is your job to "repair" or "save" other people
- Touching someone without their consent

Eleven Tips for Establishing Healthy Boundaries

Follows are some ideas to help you create appropriate limits without feeling guilty.

1. Recognize Your Value

The need to be treated with respect is at the core of every healthy limit. Knowing that your words, thoughts, and emotions are valued is essential. What you need, what you want, and how you feel are important.

When you establish limits for both yourself and everyone else, you are saying that you have value and should be treated with respect.

This act means that you also do not influence the actions or beliefs of anybody else. It's unrealistic to assume that people will treat you with respect if you don't give yourself that sense of value.

How can you ask for respect if you don't give it to yourself first? If you believe you are important and deserve respect, you are one step closer to establishing healthy limits without feeling guilty. It's not about exerting unreasonable control over others but about doing what you believe is good for yourself.

2. Make What You Desire Very Clear

Be clear about your desires and the significance they have before establishing a limit. Putting your desires and motivations down on paper may be a useful precursor to creating a boundary.

This will assist you in communicating your demands properly and staying focused when things become difficult. Some people find it helpful to plan their answers ahead of time and practice them until they are comfortable with how things will turn out.

3. Don't Be Shy about Your Demands

It is best to be precise and brief when conveying your limits. If you frame your limit using too many excuses, explanations, or apologies, you dilute its impact. Take note of the distinction between these two assertions:

> *"Hello, John. Unfortunately, I won't be able to assist you next Sunday."*
>
> *"Hello, John. I want to help with your Sunday shift, but unfortunately, I will not be available. Sorry, but my son's final soccer match is on that day. I feel obligated to support him. I'm sorry if I've offended you. I'm aware that I need to schedule things better. I could improve at remembering things."*

The second example emphasizes the impression that saying "No" is improper. Keep things straightforward and know that you deserve to request what you need without explaining.

4. Expect Opposition, but Don't Let It Dissuade You

Some individuals may react negatively if you begin imposing limits on their behavior. Those who have benefited from your lack of limitations are the least likely to encourage you to alter your approach, as they have the most to lose. It may take some time for some individuals to accept your new ways.

Avoiding disagreement is a popular excuse for not establishing limits. You put other people's comfort and happiness above your own since you wouldn't want to cause any trouble. When people don't like your limits, it's easy to revert to apathy.

However, just because others react negatively to your limits doesn't imply you shouldn't have any. You should seek assistance and take precautions to ensure your own safety. Keep in mind that each time someone pushes back against your limits, it's proof that you should probably keep them.

You have no control over how people will respond to your limits. You are under no obligation to soothe their feelings or shoulder the blame for their conduct. You are only accountable for your own thoughts and actions.

5. Setting Limits Is a Continuous Process

Rules and expectations of a parent to a child must be communicated to children regularly. Setting boundaries with adults is similar.

You may need to establish boundaries with the same individual on many occasions. And when your situation changes, you'll have to establish new limits. Constantly setting new limits is necessary.

6. Set Limits for Your Own Good, Not to Exert Dominance over Others

Boundaries are not meant to be used as exploitation or punishment. They are an important part of taking care of yourself and are an example of self-care (although others benefit too).

Setting and keeping clear boundaries in your life can help you avoid physical and mental abuse or violence and the risks that come with taking on too much, working too hard, and feeling stressed.

While wanting others to respect your space is natural, you must realize that this is not always possible. The establishment of limits serves as a declaration of identity and needs.

Your limits indicate, *"I am important." "My emotions are important." "My thoughts are important." "My health is important." "My desires are important." "My requirements are important."*

Having boundaries means standing up for yourself and your values rather than trying to get other people to bend to your will. It means you also have alternatives if people do not treat you nicely. You may emotionally and physically separate yourself.

7. Be Clear When You Interact with Others

Making sure your communication is straightforward and unambiguous will help lessen feelings of guilt. Always remember that you can request assistance when you feel you need it. In certain situations, it's okay to decline an offer. Always remember that "No" is a complete sentence and may stand on its own. Do not hesitate to say it, and remember that you do not need to explain yourself.

Maintain simplicity, clarity, and directness to avoid misinterpretation. Apologies, excuses, and explanations that aren't required or are too lengthy merely confuse the issue more. Your intended meaning may not get through to the other person. They may not take you seriously and persist in attempting to change your mind.

When you establish a limit with someone, you must know exactly what you want to accomplish. When you know exactly what you want, it's much easier to express yourself.

8. Take Note of the Repercussions of Weak Boundaries

Limits are difficult to establish, but having none at all may be more frustrating. Most people are so worried about what could go wrong or what others might think that they can't see how important it is to make real connections with other people.

Think about the things you'll be forced to give up because your limits are weak. You'll undoubtedly neglect yourself and miss out on other potential sources of happiness.

You will keep having the same issues if you don't create personal limits because you fear the worst-case possibilities.

9. Learn to Distinguish Between Healthy Limits and Selfishness

Is it selfish to have limits set up between you and others? Is your focus solely on you and what you can get from people? Are you requesting that they provide you with a service or benefit you don't deserve? Do you believe you are entitled to their resources, including their time and attention? If this describes you, your "limit" may be selfish.

Conversely, a good boundary is centered upon you. It specifies the limits of your patience and the actions you'll take if another person breaches those limits. Healthy boundaries protect you from feeling exhausted, underappreciated, and exploited. Setting limits with someone taking more than they're giving is not selfish, even when they experience negative emotions like sadness, anger, or disappointment.

Those who need help distinguishing between limits and selfishness may also confuse being pleasant with showing kindness. Those who struggle to set limits on their interactions with others will "be polite" even if they aren't feeling like it. They feel obligated to donate their time and money. Those who prioritize their wellbeing and establish proper boundaries are also able to give generously from the goodness of their hearts because their personal limitations give them more time.

10. Be with Individuals Who Respect Limits

Try to find those who are at ease with giving and receiving negative feedback. They may be anybody, from acquaintances to family members to coworkers to baristas at your neighborhood cafe.

You should give your time and focus to these individuals. Your time with them will help you recognize that setting limits is not selfish but a natural and healthy part of any relationship.

It may also demonstrate that limits do not harm good relationships. When a loving couple sets realistic limits on their relationship, they don't stop caring for one another. Anyone who stops caring because of *that* has no right to be in your life!

Although it can be frustrating to watch two people figure out how to share the same amount of space, it can also be incredibly illuminating and instructive to watch them work through this process together.

11. Apologize (If You Were Knowingly Cruel)

There's no point in feeling guilty about prioritizing your well-being. Therefore, there's no point in feeling guilty about the boundaries you've established. If you try to soften the blow of having limits, it will simply be a reflection of your vulnerability or be perceived as a weakness and will likely be met with resistance.

However, many individuals, as we all know, overreach by being extremely strict and aggressive in their boundary-setting. They keep their anger within them for years until it explodes, at which point they do far more harm to others than was required.

Perhaps you recently set a fair limit, but you may have said it with more empathy. If this is the case, it is okay to express your thoughts and apologize. Say something like, "I apologize for losing my cool yesterday." "Having this boundary established with you is crucial, but I should have said something sooner and without being rude."

Step-by-Step Guide to Conquering Guilt When Setting Limits

To begin, it will take some time before you can establish healthy limits without experiencing shame and regret. Suppose you engage in this process often enough. In that case, you will notice that the sentiments either cease emerging altogether or become weaker and shorter-lived, allowing you to get rid of them more quickly.

Before beginning this process, ensure you're setting appropriate limits and exercising compassionate distancing.

The process's end objective is straightforward; to transform your negative emotional response (anger, despair, regret, disappointment, and resentment) into a positive one (compassion, contentment, patience, and kindness).

Step One: Recognize How You Feel When Establishing Boundaries

You'll need to be aware of your present emotions to recognize the onset of feelings of remorse, humiliation, or guilt. Setting limits isn't easy, but you've got an advantage if you go into it knowing you need to.

Every thought generates some emotion. This is more difficult when the barrier is being challenged in real-time. Anger is probably the first emotion you experience when someone pushes against your boundaries, whether they do it intentionally or not. It is up to you to identify this feeling of rage and put a stop to it before it grows. Taking a minute to reflect on your present situation is crucial.

Do so without hesitation or irritation. Just give in to the emotion and let yourself experience it.

Identifying your feelings helps you set clear boundaries.
https://pixabay.com/es/photos/ni%c3%b1a-ventana-sentar-sentado-espere-5801502/

Step Two: Concentrate on Empathy Rather than Sympathy

For instance, if your closest friend's grandpa has passed away, you may feel pity for them and want to do something to help them. Every day, you may call to see how they are doing or bring them food. Of course, it is a great reaction. You go into high gear, planning out how you can improve your friend's situation or make their life easier.

However, pity is not a good reaction when establishing a boundary. Instead, it would be better if you concentrated on empathy. To be empathetic, you must be patient and understand the other person's situation without taking it on yourself.

Step Three: Stand firm

You are less likely to feel guilty if you keep your boundaries with compassion.

Reacting from a position of fear gets you into difficulty with their reaction. Therefore, you should not explain, defend, request understanding, or request permission. Instead, you may use language that sounds like this:

"I sense your disappointment at my declining your invitation to join you, but I will have to remain at home."

"You seem upset that I won't be available on Saturday. I get that, and if you give me a week's notice in the future, I'll do all I can to assist."

"I've already budgeted for my annual giving."

"I won't be able to organize the party, but I'll gladly help with the cleanup afterward."

Remember that you have no control over their responses. When expressing your needs, it is your responsibility to do so in a courteous, compassionate, and even loving way.

An important part of taking care of yourself is establishing and maintaining healthy boundaries. Healthy boundaries lead to healthy relationships.

A person who isn't used to setting limits could initially feel ashamed or selfish, but it is important for their emotional and mental health.

In conclusion, although it is essential to create limits, always respect the boundaries of those around us, including our families, romantic partners, supervisors, colleagues, and everyone else we come into contact with.

A Quiz on Personal Boundaries

To begin, close your eyes and consider the three people who you consider to be your closest family and friends. Next, construct a term to express your feelings about your relationship with them.

Then, consider the following statements in the light of your three closest relationships, and mark any that ring true. Make sure to respond with your immediate gut reaction.

Lastly, add up the totals for each section to get a sense of where you are in terms of setting and maintaining personal limits.

Weak Boundaries

☐ I prioritize other people's needs and desires before my own.

☐ To avoid controversy, I agree with everyone.

☐ I can't seem to say "No" to anything.

☐ Out of dread or shame, I'm hesitant to say "No."

☐ I let other people do the talking for me.

☐ I've come to tolerate bad behavior from others.

☐ I find myself contributing more than my fair share to the relationship.

- ☐ I attempt to "fix" other people's issues.
- ☐ I try to exert control over others.
- ☐ I don't have faith in myself or others.

Total Number Checked

Healthy Boundaries

- ☐ Without shame, I am able to establish limits to safeguard my wellbeing.
- ☐ I can communicate my honest emotions, favorable or not.
- ☐ I'm okay with other people's feelings.
- ☐ I respect people and don't try to alter or "fix" them.
- ☐ I know that disagreement is part of personal relationships.
- ☐ I'd rather quit a relationship than let someone abuse me.
- ☐ I don't adopt others' sentiments, desires, or preferences.
- ☐ I can make my own judgments and protect my interests while considering others'.
- ☐ I'm not scared to upset or annoy people with my viewpoint.
- ☐ I'm responsible for my own feelings, and others can be too.

Total Number Checked

Rigid Boundaries

- ☐ I'm annoyed when others don't share my views.
- ☐ I have trouble expressing my sentiments and hardly consider others'.
- ☐ I often use rage and intimidation to obtain what I want.
- ☐ I maintain an emotional distance from others.
- ☐ I'm uncomfortable with physical touch unless I initiate it.
- ☐ I criticize people when they do not follow my instructions.
- ☐ I won't "play" if things don't go my way.
- ☐ I get irritated if somebody uses my stuff, even if they ask.
- ☐ I expect compensation for my assistance or charity.

☐ My "space" is seldom open to others.

Total Number Checked

The section in which you checked the most boxes determines the type of limits you have. Try to accept your current situation and realize that it's alright since you're giving it your all. If you want, you can always push yourself further and make more positive changes. Consider if you would like to make any changes to your boundaries to make them more stable and healthier.

Chapter 3: How to Turn Insecurity into Confidence

Insecurity, as defined by WebMD.com, is a "feeling of inadequacy (not good enough) and uncertainty." It makes you worry about your goals, relationships, and ability to deal with certain situations.

When you suffer from insecurity, you become dependent on the viewpoints of others and lose your ability to think for yourself. Because you do not trust your own judgment, it prevents you from taking any action. When this happens, you are compelled to settle for less and are prevented from having high expectations of yourself. Therefore, if you want to overcome insecurity and become more confident, you need to learn how to trust yourself and become more assertive in your communication style.

Working on your confidence helps you overcome your insecurities and set boundaries.
https://www.pexels.com/photo/woman-wearing-blue-shawl-lapel-suit-jacket-1036622/

What Is Assertiveness

Assertiveness is a skill that, once mastered, allows you to speak with confidence and a forceful tone conveying finality in your words while remaining polite and warm. You are assertive when you stand your ground firmly and sternly defend your point of view without being aggressive. Some characteristics of an assertive person are as follows:

- They leave room for the opinions of others and can respond most appropriately, whether they agree with them or not.
- They are expressive and do not hold back their opinions about feelings, emotions, situations, circumstances, events, and happenings.
- They recognize that different points of view matter in every situation, so even though they are confident in themselves, they leave room for dissenting opinions and politely respond to them.
- As a result of their self-assurance and belief that people won't ignore them when they speak, they speak with confidence.
- They appreciate other people for their actions and contributions. They are aware of other people's contributions and are not hesitant to recognize them when appropriate. They do not feel sad when someone else is praised or commended around them.
- They accept responsibility for their actions and decisions and maintain a consistent position over time.
- They do not deny their human frailty and thus are quick to own up to their mistakes and errors and apologize when necessary.
- Though assertive people trust themselves and are very confident in their opinions and convictions, they do not regard themselves highly in comparison to others. They recognize the importance of others around them.
- They have self-control, which is reflected in their personality. They control their emotions when necessary and express them effectively when required. Assertiveness assists you in becoming the master of your circumstances.

You can train yourself to be more assertive, which is a very positive development. After gaining an understanding of the qualities that define an assertive person, you can say with complete certainty that you admire the characteristic. In the following paragraphs, we will talk about various approaches that can help you develop your assertiveness.

How to Become More Assertive

To become more assertive, you must first acknowledge that you have room for improvement. As soon as you accept this, the next step is to formulate a plan for how to proceed with your journey toward assertiveness. Increasing your assertiveness can be accomplished through the following steps:

Start with Where You Are

Even though you have a picture in your head of the person you ultimately want to be, you have to start from where you are and build up from there. Never feel ashamed or embarrassed about taking tiny steps toward improving yourself. Next, you have to come to terms with the fact that you'll err. When something like this occurs, try not to let it dishearten you. Rather, focus on how far you've come and be proud of your progress.

Practice Self-Appraisal

Take the time to examine yourself and your attitude, identify areas that need improvement, and begin working on them. How often do you speak up instead of remaining silent and allowing others' opinions to overshadow your own? Are you afraid of disappointing people or saying "no" to them? Do you accept responsibility for your actions or easily shift blame to others? Do you allow people to express themselves freely around you, or do you always let your opinion take precedence?

Determine which areas of your life require improvement and work hard to improve them. One way to ensure you're making progress is to ask yourself honestly how you feel after each interaction with others. Were you relieved and relaxed? Did you feel like something was missing, or did you want to go back and make some changes? If this is the case, it indicates that you could have performed better in some areas.

While it is impossible to reverse the situation, you should note the errors you want to correct and ensure they do not occur again in subsequent interactions. When you continue to make these corrections over time, you'll progress from one level to the next, and your progress will be evident.

Be Confident

When you have an opinion about something or have made a decision about it, communicate it as though it were your decision and belief, and have the courage to say that it is yours. Master the art of making frequent use of the word *"I."* *"I want to do this,"* *"I don't think this is right,"* and *"I will not be able to attend the meeting due to other commitments."* *"I want to do this,"* *"I don't think this is right."*

Learn to Say "No"

Most of the time, we try our hardest to please others and avoid disappointing them, even when it is inconvenient, which begins to impact our schedules, and we end up with many unfinished tasks or missed deadlines, reducing our credibility and integrity.

As a result, you must accept disappointing people as a part of life and say "no" when you believe you cannot meet whatever demand is placed before you. It could be a request for your time, money, attention, professional services, or something else. Learn to say "no" when necessary. You can accompany it with an apology or explanation to help the person understand and not take offense, but you do not always need to.

Use Your Body Language

When communicating with others, use gestures to complement your words. Gestures demonstrate that you are confident and focused on the subject at hand. Make gestures with your hands, eyes, head, and any other body part that you can use. Some people may not recall your exact words, but they will remember your actions. This is the communication power of audiovisuals. Make eye contact with your listeners or audience on occasion. Maintain your posture and speak with confidence at all times. Practice in a mirror or ask some of your friends to listen to you and provide honest feedback.

Master Your Emotions

You will need to learn how to manage your emotions and keep them in check. Recognize when you are likely to have an emotional outburst and withdraw from such situations until you are relieved. Allowing your feelings to get in the way of a conversation or other interaction will harm your confidence. Don't let your emotions undermine your self-esteem.

Advantages of Being Assertive

Assertiveness is beneficial in many ways. For example, it will help people understand you better. You will be able to communicate your needs and wants, emotions and opinions, and your stance and decisions to others. As a result, they will be able to understand you properly.

People respect you when you are assertive, and you respect them and their opinions because you are not aggressive. This act strengthens your relationships with others while also increasing your confidence. When you are assertive, you control your life and your environment, deciding what kind of environment you want to work in.

Psychological Tricks to Look More Confident

While you work on developing your confidence, which is a long-term process, you should immediately begin practicing some tricks to make you appear more confident and secure in yourself. Some of these are as follows:

- As soon as negative thoughts enter your mind, replace them with the opposite. Speak encouraging words to yourself and reassure yourself of your courage and confidence. *"I can do it, I am a bold speaker, and people want to listen to me."* As you do this regularly, these thoughts become a part of you and help reprogram your mind to think positively.

- When expressing yourself, use firm words. These are specific and very direct, rather than phrases like *"I believe"* or *"I am not sure."* When you're not sure, don't say them, but when you are, be firm in expressing your certainty. This attitude will boost your confidence and allow you to be more assertive when communicating with others. Remove any extraneous words or phrases from your communication.

- Avoid time wasters such as activities that are irrelevant to you. Social media can be very addictive, and you should be wary of the amount of time you spend on it. Social media tends to make you compare yourself to others who appear to be doing better than you, putting undue pressure on you. Understand that you owe it to yourself to do better than you did the day before, not to do better than anyone else. This exercise keeps you on your toes when it comes to personal development.

- Dress smartly and confidently. Dressing well gives you the self-assurance you need to face people without feeling down or inferior, which is why you should prioritize your physical appearance. Look good, feel good.

How to Improve Your Posture

Before we discuss how to improve your posture, it is important to understand that there are two types of posture: dynamic and static. Dynamic pose refers to how you carry yourself while moving; for example, while walking, running, jogging, or playing. Static posture refers to how you support yourself while in a certain position; for example, sitting on a couch, working at your desk, having a drink at a bar, and so on.

Improving your posture begins by paying attention to your spine and being aware of it whenever you are moving or in a position. Check that your head is not bowed and that your shoulders are straight above your hips. Stretch your neck backward from time to time to allow the straightening of your neck curves, and try some yoga positions to improve your posture.

Your posture goes a long way in giving off a confident appearance.
https://www.pexels.com/photo/man-and-woman-smiling-inside-building-1367269/

Exercise frequently to help your body become more flexible. Yoga, for example, is an exercise that can help you straighten your posture.

Put on good, comfortable shoes. They help you to maintain good walking posture. High heels are nice, but consider wearing them less often. Just make sure you're comfortable and upright when you're on the go.

Have a comfortable workspace where you don't have to stretch to type or write. Check that your table is not too high or too low and your chair is correctly positioned. Because you spend most of your time at your desk, if your chair and table are not in a good and comfortable position, it will cause you pain and potentially some defects in your posture over time.

Ways to Automate Assertiveness

Over time, the qualities of our character that have been learned become ingrained in us. No longer is it necessary for us to make a concerted effort to remember or pay attention to them. Because we are so used to them, we now perform them automatically, which is exactly what it means to say that a process has been automated.

As you work on developing your assertiveness, you'll find that it gradually becomes a part of you, and, as a result, you won't require as much practice to demonstrate it. What are the steps involved in reaching this level of automation?

Stay Consistent

The first step toward automating a process is ensuring consistency. When you are consistent in your practice of everything we have discussed, it will eventually work its way into your subconscious. It's possible that you won't realize it until after you've been able to demonstrate it consistently without needing to practice or consciously remember it.

Avoid Fillers in Your Conversation

Learn and practice speaking for an extended period without including unnecessary fillers in your speech. It improves your coordination while also boosting your confidence. There is a significant distinction between thinking and speaking. The first allows for jumbled thoughts and events. In contrast, the second requires a more coordinated expression in which you do not have to repeat certain things over and over, nor will it be appropriate to punctuate your speech with unnecessary and irrelevant words.

Practice mental rehearsals regarding public speaking. Experiment with it by speaking to yourself in a mirror, then speak aloud and ask your friends and family to rate your performance. Practice produces better results.

Avoid the Use of Uncultured Words

Even when you're in a bad mood, avoiding the use of uncultured words will keep you one step ahead of the game. Resist the urge to use derogatory words. Instead, focus on finding more effective ways to deal with any situation. Always keep your audience in mind and figure out the most effective way to communicate with them.

Use a different strategy for everyone, as failure to do so may backfire. Comprehension levels vary, and so should your mode of communication. When you understand your audience and address them appropriately, you send the message that you are confident in what you are doing, which boosts people's confidence in you and, thus, your own level of confidence.

Set Goals

Setting and sticking to goals is beneficial. It could be learning new postures, expanding your vocabulary, changing your wardrobe, or making new friends. Overall, ensure you have goals that will help you to gain confidence and assertiveness. You can confide in someone you trust and be accountable to them. It will help you stay on track when you have someone to whom you report.

The journey from a point in your life where you are unsure of your capabilities and strengths to a point where you can walk with your head held high can be an exciting and adventurous experience. You can expect that it will be both rewarding and difficult. At times, you may feel like giving up and letting everything slide. After all, who cares how you carry yourself, right?

You must have identified reasons to value assertiveness. It helps you to transition from a state of irresponsibility to discipline. Your confidence level rises when you become assertive and aware of your body language as you interact with others. Determine which aspects of your life require improvement and begin working on them. Feel free to start small or to make mistakes. Mistakes are a natural part of life and teach us what does not work.

Be open to criticism, especially from trusted friends and family members who always give you honest feedback as you improve. Never make fun of yourself because it allows you to criticize yourself as you improve constructively. As you progress, wear your confidence like a badge of honor and ensure your body language matches your words.

Do not always make yourself available to others. Understand when to say "yes" and when to say "no" and never feel guilty about it. Accept what you are certain you can do and avoid taking on what you cannot.

Be in control of your emotions. Do your best to keep your feelings in check so you don't have to apologize for your lack of self-control. Always be mindful of your words - this is the primary criteria by which people judge you and your primary means of expression. You may be surprised at how far you've come if you put into practice the things that we've talked about and figure out how to include them in your day-to-day activities. The following set of review questions is intended to help you to retain information from this conversation. You are free to take as much time as you need to adapt them to your specific circumstances. If you can't find anything better, just make do with these and monitor your progress.

Assessment Questions

1. Reflect and fill the spaces below on the areas of your life where you have shown signs of insecurity

_____

_____

_____

2. From what you have learned, are you willing to take the necessary action? Yes/ No (only continue with the assessment if you ticked the "Yes" option.)

3. Mention some specific actions you'll take to improve the areas mentioned above.

_____

_____

_____

4. I will be accountable to _____ (fill in the name of a friend or loved one who would be responsible for your progress).

5. Signature _____

It is helpful to date this, so you can check on your progress over time.

Chapter 4: 6 Mistakes That Ruin Your Love Life

When you meet someone and fall in love, you want to think the best of them. You want to believe that you have finally met "the one," so you ignore certain incidents and tell-tale signs and convince yourself that the other person didn't mean to do something or that they have your best interest at heart. However, some relationships can become toxic, even if they don't start out this way, while other types of relationships are abusive from the beginning, especially if the person you are dating is a narcissist. Whether your partner has toxic traits or not, a lack of boundaries can turn a healthy relationship into an abusive and codependent one.

Setting boundaries from the beginning is a great foundation for a healthy relationship.
https://pixabay.com/es/photos/rom%c3%a1ntico-abrazo-uni%c3%b3n-conectividad-1934223/

According to the author and psychotherapist David Richo, setting boundaries doesn't mean abandoning your partner but allows you to have a healthy relationship while maintaining your independence and identity. Boundaries balance and strengthen relationships as they allow both partners' involvement rather than one leading and the other following. Unconditional love and boundaries can co-exist. A person should have the right to decide how they want to be treated. Many people in toxic relationships lose themselves as they sacrifice their needs in order to please their partners. When the relationship ends, they feel lost as they let themselves be defined by the other person.

Think of how great it would feel to be in a relationship where you give as much as you take, and your partner makes you a priority like you make them and cares about your needs. Imagine being in a relationship where your voice is heard and your opinion matters just like theirs. You can only achieve that by choosing how you want to be treated and setting healthy boundaries. You can have a healthy relationship without betraying who you are and your values.

This chapter will open your eyes to red flags or mistakes in relationships that you shouldn't allow and provide you with tips to set healthy boundaries so you can have a happy and long relationship.

Mistake #1: Your Partner Tries to Change You

Your partner will not be straightforward about wanting you to change; they will be subtle. It usually comes out in controlling behavior, gaslighting, criticism, or mockery that makes you question yourself or shakes your confidence. You will end up changing to please them or to avoid conflict. There are certain signs and behaviors that show your partner is trying to change you. This isn't something you should ignore, and it must be addressed right away.

Signs Your Partner Is Trying to Change You
Comparing You to Other People

When your partner wants you to change something, they will compare you to someone else, such as a friend or even an ex. This is a tactic to flatten your confidence and manipulate you to do something they want. For instance, if your boyfriend wants you to stop putting on heavy makeup, they will tell you, "All my exes kept their makeup natural," or point at an actress and say, "Look how beautiful she looks with simple makeup. I don't understand why you do this to yourself."

Changing Your Personal Style

If your partner has a negative opinion about your clothes, hairstyle, makeup, or appearance in general, they are trying to change your style. If you wear skinny jeans, they will tell you they prefer dresses. If you put on pink nail polish, they will tell you bolder colors are sexier. Your personal style is part of your identity, and no one should dictate what you wear.

Undermining Your Career

"Really, you are a food blogger? So you just write about food? What do you contribute to society?" Or "Working from home is easy." Nowadays, many people work from home and work as hard as those who work from an office. A loving partner should never undermine your career but respect and support you while you are doing what you are passionate about.

Doesn't Like Your Friends

Unless your friends are alcoholics, drug addicts, or criminals, your partner doesn't have the right to tell you who you should or shouldn't spend your time with. If your partner constantly mocks and ridicules your friends, they are trying to make you spend more time with them and their friends instead. The biggest red flag here is when they give an ultimatum "your friends or me." This is a clear sign that your partner wants to change you and control your behavior. Your partner will be more persistent if your friends notice how you have changed. In fact, when your friends make comments about how you haven't been yourself lately, you should take notice. Close friends are usually the first to notice when something is off about you, so you should listen to them and self-reflect.

Rewarding Behavior

If you change yourself for your partner, they will reward this behavior either by bringing you gifts or showering you with compliments. For instance, "I told you short hair would look better on you" or "I told you we'd have more fun staying home. You look happier."

Your partner is either:
- toxic and is trying to change you to exert control, OR
- they aren't aware of their behavior

Setting boundaries will help you tell the difference. If your partner isn't a narcissist, they can respect your boundaries. However, this will not happen right away. Establishing boundaries in relationships usually takes time for both of you to get used to the new rhythm of your relationship. If your partner is a narcissist or toxic, they will not respect your boundaries.

Setting Boundaries

It is essential to be calm when you address your partner's controlling behavior. Talk to them calmly and help them see things from your perspective. There is a reason behind everything. Try to understand why your partner has to comment and criticize everything you say and do. Does this stem from their childhood? Did their parents try to control them by dictating what they should wear and who they should spend time with? Don't treat the conversation as an interrogation, be empathetic and have an open dialogue with them. In some cases, your partner will lose their temper or deny their behavior so try to remain calm and understanding. There is a chance they aren't aware of their behavior. Be gentle and explain that the constant need to change you comes off as controlling.

Set boundaries by telling them how you want to be treated, like respecting your style and choices in friends. Take back control. Stop trying to please them by dressing the way they like or cutting off your friends. Live your life and do the things you like. Whether it's a job you want to apply to or a haircut, don't give in to their controlling behavior. Your partner's attempt to change you can destroy your self-confidence, so surround yourself with friends who will remind you of your worth. Stand up for yourself if they try to belittle your job or friends. Your partner may be resistant to your boundaries at first, which is to be expected. Keep sticking to your boundaries to send a message that you are serious about them. If they keep pushing your boundaries, you can either consider couple therapy or leave them.

Mistake #2: Compromising Too Much

Naturally, you want to make your partner happy because you love them. However, a lack of boundaries can make you please your partner to the extent of giving up your own values or mental wellbeing. Compromising is a normal part of any relationship. Sometimes you give up something, while at other times, they do. There is balance and cooperation from both sides. However, in some cases, you may find yourself giving up your identity or values to make them happy. For instance, you are a vegetarian, but your husband enjoys going on hunting trips. He loves to keep souvenirs from the animals he hunts at home, but this really makes you uncomfortable. You talk to him about it, but he dismisses you or belittles your lifestyle choices. After constant fighting, he threatens to leave you, so you decide to make peace and accept him hanging animal trophies around the house and even listen and laugh at his hunting stories to avoid another fight.

However, this can be damaging to your mental health. You will feel guilty for giving up on your values and feel resentment toward yourself and your partner. Suppressing your feelings will not work, as this will lead to a blow up because of bottled-up anger and resentment. Constant fighting and conflicts will push your partner away, leading you to sacrifice and give up more to please them. It is a vicious circle.

Signs You Are Compromising Too Much in Your Relationship
Second-Guessing Your Decisions

According to sex and intimacy coach Irene Fehr, second-guessing every decision you make is a clear sign that you aren't satisfied with your choices. For instance, your partner wants to move to a new city, but you don't. After a few arguments, you agree just to keep the peace and make him/her happy. However, if you keep going back and forth and replaying the argument in your head, it is a sign you aren't happy with your decision.

Losing Your Identity

Compare your relationships before and after you met your partner. Do you still have the same friends, interests, independence, and values? If you don't feel like yourself anymore, you may have given up too much. You will find yourself living your partner's life and doing what they like instead of what you enjoy.

If this is a pattern in your relationship where you compromise your identity and your values to please your partner or to avoid fighting, take a step now and set boundaries.

Setting Boundaries
Make a List

Understand you can't compromise on everything. Make a list of things you'll never compromise on and communicate it with your partner so you can be on the same page.

Say No

If your partner is asking you to give up your values, happiness, or something significant to you, say "no." Be assertive and make it clear that there is nothing they can say to change your mind; no means no.

Demand Respect

Your partner should respect your needs and values just like you respect theirs. They shouldn't act like your needs and beliefs don't matter.

Mistake #3: They Can't Handle Conflict

The ability to handle conflict shows maturity. Conflict is a natural part of relationships— all couples argue and disagree. Your partner's actions and reactions during a conflict will show you whether your relationship is healthy or not.

Signs Your Partner Handles Conflict Badly

Storming Off

Does this happen? Instead of sitting and talking things out, your partner storms off whenever you have a conflict or try to communicate your feelings. This usually happens when you call them out on their bad or toxic behavior, and they don't want to admit they are in the wrong.

Raising Their Voice

If your partner is in a weak position, they will raise their voice to manipulate you or scare you, so you let things go. In some difficult situations, partners can use insults or be hostile and violent.

Giving You the Silent Treatment

Narcissists and toxic individuals hate it when you point out their mistakes or flaws. They will punish you by giving you the silent treatment to scare you from ever speaking up again. Next time they do something that upsets you, you'll keep it to yourself to avoid this passive-aggressive behavior.

Turning the Table

If your partner constantly turns the table to avoid being held accountable for their mistakes, it is a clear sign of their inability to handle conflict.

Although you can't control your partner's reaction, make it clear that the way they handle conflict isn't acceptable or respectable.

Setting Boundaries

Sit down with your partner when you are both calm, not during an argument, and agree on the best strategies to handle conflict. For instance, you can create a list of rules and save it on your phone. You can add things like;

- No threats
- No storming off
- No name-calling or insults
- No loud voices
- No pointing fingers
- No throwing things
- No yelling
- No interruptions

Make it clear that you aren't fighting each other or pointing fingers but trying to find a solution to a problem. You are on the same team. If your partner doesn't abide by the rules, walk away from the conversation. For instance, if they raise their voice or insult you, walk away to make it clear that you don't accept this behavior. This situation is different from them storming off during an argument. They walked away because they couldn't handle conflict, but you didn't accept disrespect. Give yourself space to calm down and tell them you will not tolerate that behavior again.

Mistake #4: They Don't Take Responsibility for Their Actions

An immature partner will never take responsibility for their behavior, which usually shows in how they handle conflict.

Signs Your Partner Refuses to Take Responsibility

Nothing Is Their Fault

An irresponsible partner will blame you, other people, family members, the weather, the government, or anyone or anything but themselves. For instance, your partner said some hurtful things during an argument. Instead of owning up to their actions and apologizing, they will blame it on being stressed at work or having a bad day or will blame you for driving them to act this way. They will say, "You made me raise my voice" or "I was drunk; I didn't know what I was saying." Simply put, they are always the victims.

They Refuse to Change

Taking responsibility for your actions means you are willing to change. If your partner apologizes after they upset you, but their behavior remains the same, they aren't willing to change. An apology is a promise that they will never repeat a specific behavior again. If they keep going back to their same old ways, their apology is meaningless.

Setting Boundaries

Don't accept your partner's blame or accusations when they try to avoid responsibility. If you are in a codependent relationship, you'll be fixing their mistakes or constantly apologizing for their behavior and making excuses for them to other people. Stand your ground and refuse to be their scapegoat. Don't accept apologies unless they show you they will change. Be prepared to walk away if you feel they aren't willing to grow up and own up to their mistakes.

Mistake #5: Excessive Jealousy

A little jealousy is normal. For instance, it is normal to get jealous if your partner's ex is texting them. However, jealousy that leads to controlling behavior is toxic. They will dictate what you wear, look through your phone, or show up when you are out with friends to spy on you. Extreme jealousy is unhealthy, and it usually stems from your partner's lack of self-confidence.

Signs Your Partner Is Extremely Jealous

- They make a big deal whenever you spend time with your friends.
- They call you and text you all day to ask who you are with and what you are doing.
- They have issues with your good-looking friends because they worry you'll cheat.
- They control what you wear.
- They look through your phone.

Setting Boundaries
Prevent Them from Looking through Your Phone

Under no circumstances is your partner allowed to look through your phone or your things. Just asking to read your text messages or check your photo gallery is a big red flag. Make it clear that this isn't acceptable, and if they don't trust you, you have a bigger issue. If they pressure you, say "No" and stand your ground.

Have a Conversation

Talk to them and get to the root of their jealousy. Is it a lack of self-confidence, lack of trust, or has someone cheated on them before?

Ask Them to Trust You

After finding out where their jealousy issue comes from, ask them to try to trust you. Tell them they don't have to text you every five minutes when you are out with friends or get to know every detail of your life to do that. Talk about trust and tell them that they should trust you as you trust them. You can try couple therapy to help them work on their trust issues.

Mistake #6: Discussing Relationships with Others

Partners should work on solving their problems together, not with other people. If your partner runs to their friends with all your relationship issues and shares your most intimate secrets with them, they don't respect you or your privacy. It is normal to talk about your partner or relationship with your friends but sharing every detail with them, including every fight you have and personal things about your partner, isn't acceptable. If you feel that you are dating your partner and their friends, it is time to set boundaries.

Setting Boundaries

Have a calm conversation with your partner and explain there are things they shouldn't share with their friends. Relationship problems and intimate details should stay between you two. Make it clear that this has created trust issues, and you will not be able to trust them if everything you say is reported to their friends. If your partner can't stop themselves, stop sharing any private information or secrets with them. Explain to them that it hurts your feelings when you feel you can't share things with them because you can't trust them.

Toxic Relationship Scenarios and Solutions

Problem

You tell your partner you are going out with your friends tonight, but your partner gets angry and accuses you of spending all your time with your friends and not enough time with them. They tell you they miss you when you aren't around and want to be with you all the time.

Solutions

In healthy relationships, partners don't spend all their time together. It is healthy to spend time apart. Your partner's behavior here is controlling and possessive. Explain to them that spending time with your friends doesn't mean you don't love them. Tell them it is healthy for the two of you to spend time with other people. Don't give in to your partner's demands and go out with your friends. Calmly make it clear that they can't control who you spend their time with.

Problem

You have been dating your partner for a few months, and they want you to move in together. You love your partner, but you aren't ready for this step. However, they don't want to listen to you and give you an ultimatum: either move in or the relationship is over.

Solution

Let your partner know that you love them and you definitely plan to move in, but you aren't ready for this step now. If they insist, then make it clear that this is your final decision, and they should respect your choice. If they give you an ultimatum, tell them that this isn't a healthy way to handle conflict and you are willing to talk when they are ready to have a mature conversation.

In some cases, no matter what you do, your partner will be resistant to your boundaries. If you give up hope that they will ever change, consider walking away to protect your mental health and identity.

Questions to Reflect On

- Is it appropriate for your partners to criticize your personal appearance?

- Should you give up spending time with each person your partner has an issue with?
- Should you give in to your partner's demands to avoid conflict?
- Is it acceptable for your partner to check on you every ten minutes when you are out with friends?

Boundaries can make or break your relationship. Set boundaries early on to guarantee that you and your partner are on the same page. Boundaries are necessary for all types of relationships, including family members. If you have a parent or a sibling who is manipulative, set a few rules to protect your mental health. The next chapter will provide you with healthy methods to deal with unhealthy family members.

Chapter 5: Ten Effective Ways to Deal with Difficult Family Members

We all know that feeling. You're at a family gathering, and suddenly you feel your blood pressure rising. Your heart starts to race, and you can feel the anger bubbling up inside of you. You might try to take a few deep breaths and calm down, but before long, you're in the middle of a heated argument with a family member. If this sounds familiar, you may need to work on setting healthy boundaries with your family.

Most of us have that one family member. You know the one. The one who is always asking for money, or wants to borrow your car, or is constantly asking personal questions that make you uncomfortable. We all have our boundaries - things that we don't want others to cross - but it can be difficult to assert those boundaries with family members. After all, they're family, and we want to be able to help them out. But it's important to remember that you have a right to say "no" and that it's okay to set boundaries with family members.

Learn how to set boundaries in an effective way with difficult family members.
https://pixabay.com/es/photos/pareja-discutiendo-desacuerdo-6471113/

Role of Boundaries in Family Relationships

Just as a country has borders to define its territory, so too do families have boundaries to define their members and roles. Family boundaries help to delineate who is part of the family and who is not, as well as what roles each member plays. Perhaps the most important function of family boundaries is providing a sense of stability and security. In a world that is ever-changing, family boundaries help to provide constancy in our lives. They remind us of who we are and where we belong. Additionally, family boundaries can help to reduce conflict by clarifying expectations and roles. When everyone knows what is expected of them, there is less room for misunderstanding. Finally, family boundaries can provide a sense of protection from the outside world. They can offer a safe haven from the stresses of work or school, and they can provide support during times of hardship. In short, family boundaries play an essential role in maintaining healthy relationships.

Why Managing Boundaries Can Be as Troublesome as It Is Gratifying

Family relationships can be some of the most rewarding and fulfilling connections we have in our lives. But they can also be some of the most challenging, especially when it comes to managing boundaries. Whether setting boundaries with our parents, children, or siblings, it's important to remember that these relationships are built on a foundation of love and respect. And while it can be difficult to establish clear boundaries, doing so can ultimately help to strengthen and improve our relationships.

One of the most common challenges we face when managing boundaries in family relationships is dealing with our own emotions. We may feel guilty or anxious about setting limits with our loved ones. We may worry that we're being too demanding or that we're not doing enough. It's important to remember that these feelings are natural and normal, but they shouldn't prevent us from establishing healthy boundaries.

Another common challenge is dealing with others' emotions. We may find ourselves constantly accommodating other people's needs and wants, even when it means compromising our own wellbeing. This can be a difficult habit to break, but it's important to remember that we are not responsible for other people's happiness. We can only control our own choices and actions.

Ultimately, managing boundaries in family relationships is a process of trial and error. There will be times when we make mistakes and times when our boundaries are challenged. But by remaining open and honest with ourselves and our loved ones, we can create stronger, healthier relationships built on mutual respect and understanding.

How to Implement Boundaries in a Family Relationship

1. Put Your Needs First

Boundary setting is a skill that not many of us are taught while growing up. We learn how to share, be polite, and listen to others, but we don't always learn how to put our needs first or say "no" in a way that feels good. This can leave us feeling overwhelmed, resentful, and guilty when we do try to set boundaries with family members. One way to set healthy boundaries with family members is to put your needs first. This means you make decisions based on what is best for you, not on what will make other people happy. For example, if you have a family member who is always asking for money, you can set a boundary by saying that you are not going to lend them any more money. This doesn't mean that you don't care about them. It just means that you are putting your needs first.

It can also be helpful to set boundaries around time and energy. For example, if you have a family member who always wants to talk on the phone for hours, you can set a boundary by saying that you only have 20 minutes to talk. This lets them know that you value your time and that they need to respect your time limits.

Lastly, it's important to communicate your boundaries in a clear and concise way. This means being assertive and speaking up for yourself. It's okay to be polite, but it's also okay to be firm about your needs. If you have a family member who is always making demands on your time, you can say something like, *"I love spending time with you, but I also need some time for myself. I'm happy to talk on the phone for 20 minutes, but after that, I'm going to take some time for myself."*

When we think about setting boundaries, we often focus on what we shouldn't do, such as saying "no" to requests, setting limits on our time, or asking others to respect our privacy. However, it's just as important to consider what we should do in order to set healthy boundaries. One of the most important things we can do is to put our needs first.

Setting healthy boundaries with family members can be challenging, but it's important to remember that you have a right to put yourself first. By being clear about your needs and communicating assertively, you can set boundaries in a way that feels good for everyone involved.

Of course, putting your needs first doesn't mean being completely selfish. It's important to strike a balance between taking care of yourself and taking care of others. But when setting boundaries, remember that you don't owe anyone anything beyond what you're comfortable giving. Your time, energy, and resources are yours to spend as you see fit.

2. Be Direct and Kind in Your Approach

Family relationships are some of the most important in our lives, but they can also be some of the most challenging. One difficulty that often arises is setting healthy boundaries with family members. This can be a delicate task, as you want to maintain a close relationship while still respecting your own needs and space. There are many ways to approach this, but one that can be effective is to be both direct and kind in your communication. It is important to be clear about what your needs are and what you are comfortable with, but it is also crucial to frame this in a way that shows you still care about and value the relationship. Sometimes you may need to set boundaries with family members who are overly critical, manipulative, or dismissive. It's important to remember that you don't have to put up with disrespectful treatment just because someone is related to you. If a family member repeatedly crosses your boundaries, it may be necessary to limit or end contact with that person. Here are some tips for setting boundaries in a healthy way:

- Express your feelings in a non-blaming way. For example, you might say, *"I feel hurt when you criticize me."*
- Make it clear what behavior is not acceptable. For example, you might say, *"I don't appreciate being yelled at."*
- Be assertive, but avoid being confrontational. For example, you could say, *"I'm going to take a break from this conversation,"* or *"I need some time alone."*
- State your needs clearly and firmly. For example, you might say, *"I need you to respect my decision."*
- Give yourself time to cool off if the situation feels too heated. You can always come back to the conversation later when everyone is calm.
- You could say something like, *"I love spending time with you, but I really need some space right now. I hope you understand."*

It's important to remember that setting boundaries are not about making other people happy – it's about taking care of yourself. By being direct and kind in your approach, you can set healthy boundaries with family members while still maintaining respectful relationships.

3. Value Your Time, and Request the Same from Others

Everyone has different comfort levels when it comes to setting boundaries with family members. For some, it may feel natural to share everything with their loved ones. Others may prefer to keep certain aspects of their lives private. There is no right or wrong way to approach boundary-setting. The most important thing is to respect your own needs and preferences. One way to set healthy boundaries with family members is to value your time and request the same from others. If you don't want to be interrupted while you're working, let your loved ones know in advance and ask them to respect your space. You can also set aside specific times for catch-ups rather than being available at all hours of the day. This will help you to avoid feeling overwhelmed or like you're always on duty.

It can be difficult to set boundaries with family members, especially if you have traditionally been the "go-to" person in your family. However, it is important to remember that you have a right to request the same level of respect for your time as other family members. For example, if you are only available for phone calls on Monday and Wednesday evenings, let your family know in advance and stick to that schedule. If someone asks for a last-minute favor that will require you to drop everything and change your plans, explain that you are unable to do so. It is also important to be clear about what you are willing to do for others. By setting healthy boundaries and respecting your own time, you're sending the message that you're worthy of respect from others. Family relationships can be complex and challenging, but setting healthy boundaries is key to maintaining a healthy and supportive bond with your loved ones.

Avoiding family gossip is one way to set healthy boundaries with family members. Family gossip can be hurtful and destructive, and it often leads to arguments and hard feelings. It can also be a way for family members to control and manipulate one another. If you find yourself in a situation where family members are gossiping, try to steer the conversation in another direction. You can also politely excuse yourself from the conversation. You may also want to consider setting a policy with your family that you will not tolerate gossip. Setting healthy boundaries with family members is important for maintaining a good relationship with them. It can be difficult to do, but it's worth it in the long run. By setting these boundaries, you can help to create a more positive and healthy relationship with your family.

4. Learn to Say "No"

One way to set healthy boundaries with family members is to learn to say "No." This can be difficult, especially if you have been raised to believe that you should always do what your elders or family members ask of you. However, it is important to remember that you are an adult and have the right to make your own decisions. You may need to practice saying "No" in front of a mirror or with a trusted friend before you are able to do it with a family member. But once you learn how, sticking to your boundaries will be much easier.

Here are a few possible scenarios where you might need to say "No":

- Your parents want you to visit them every weekend, but you have other plans.

- Your brother asks to borrow money from you, but you can't afford it.
- Your cousin wants you to babysit her kids, but you're not comfortable doing that.
- Your aunt asks you why you're not married yet or when you're going to have children.

If any of these things happen, just politely say "No" and give a brief explanation if necessary. For example, if your parents ask why you're not visiting them every weekend, you could say that you need some time for yourself and that you'll visit them soon. If your brother asks to borrow money from you, tell him that you don't have any extra cash right now but offer to help him in another way, like by lending him something he needs or offering to do something for him. And if your cousin asks you to babysit her kids, explain that you're not comfortable doing that but offer to do something else with them instead. Remember, it's okay to say "No" - just be polite about it!

Now let's assess your knowledge so far:

- Why is it important to learn how to say "No"?
- What are some possible scenarios where you might need to use this skill?
- How can you practice saying "No"?
- What should you do if someone gets mad at you for saying "No"?

5. Identify and Eliminate or Avoid Triggers

One way to set healthy boundaries with family members is to identify and eliminate or avoid triggers. What are the things that set you off? Is it certain topics of conversation? Is it around certain people? Once you know what your triggers are, you can either avoid them altogether or be prepared to deal with them in a healthy way. For example, if you know that discussing politics with your uncle always ends in an argument, you could decide to avoid the topic altogether. Or, if you know that being around your cousin always makes you feel anxious, you could make it a point to spend less time with her.

Of course, avoiding triggers isn't always possible. In those cases, it's important to have some tools to deal with them in a healthy way. One tool is to set limits on how much time you're willing to spend discussing triggering topics or being around triggering people. For example, you could decide that you're only going to discuss politics with your uncle for 15 minutes before changing the subject. Or you may decide that you'll only spend an hour with your cousin at family gatherings. Another tool is to practice some basic self-care techniques, such as deep breathing or positive self-talk, before and during triggering situations. This can help you to stay calm and focused on handling the situation in a healthy way.

So far, we've talked about ways to avoid or deal with triggers in triggering situations. But what about when those situations arise unexpectedly? In those cases, it's important to be able to excuse yourself from the situation if necessary. This might mean leaving the room if someone starts arguing with you or taking a break from socializing if you start feeling overwhelmed. It's also important to have an exit plan for situations that are especially triggering for you - like dreaded holiday gatherings - so that you can leave if necessary without feeling guilty or like you're letting someone down.

By now, you should understand what it takes to set healthy boundaries with family members, but let's recap. First, identify your triggers. Secondly, eliminate or avoid them if possible. Thirdly, set limits on time spent in triggering situations. Fourth, practice some self-care techniques, and fifth, have an exit plan for particularly triggering situations. Lastly, remember that it's okay to excuse yourself from any situation - even if it's in the middle of dinner! - if it means taking care of yourself.

6. Be Assertive

It can be really tough to set boundaries with family members, especially if you have a close relationship with them. You don't want to hurt their feelings or come across as being too harsh, but you need to protect yourself and your own wellbeing. One way to set healthy boundaries with family members is to be assertive by using "I" statements. For example, instead of saying, "You're always criticizing me, and it's really getting on my nerves," try saying something like, "I feel hurt and disrespected when you criticize me. Can we please talk about this in a more constructive way?" By using "I" statements, you're owning your feelings and making it clear that you're not prepared to put up with disrespectful behavior. This technique takes practice, but it's worth it for the sake of your mental health. Another example is instead of saying, "You're always interrupting me," you could say, "I need to finish my thought." This sends the message that you're not willing to tolerate being interrupted, but you're also not attacking the person. You can also ask your family members questions to get them to understand your perspective. For example, you could say, "Can you see how that may be hurtful?" By doing this, you're not only setting a boundary but also helping your family members to see things from your perspective. So, next time you're feeling overwhelmed by a family member, remember to be assertive.

7. Learn to Walk Away

Setting healthy boundaries with family members can be difficult, but it's important to ensure that your relationships are positive and supportive. One way to do this is to learn to walk away. This doesn't mean you have to cut off all communication or never see them again, but it does mean learning when it's time to take a break.

There are a few different scenarios where this may be necessary. Maybe you have a family member who is always putting you down or making you feel bad about yourself. Or perhaps there's someone who is constantly asking for favors but never reciprocates. In these situations, it's important to recognize when you need some time for yourself.

You may also need to walk away if a situation is becoming too heated or if you're starting to feel uncomfortable. It's okay to say that you need some time to calm down or that you need to leave. This can be tricky if the person isn't respecting your wishes, but it's important to stick to your guns. Finally, sometimes it's just not possible or healthy to maintain a relationship with a certain family member. If someone is abusive, for example, it's probably best to cut ties completely.

Do you think you could benefit from learning how to walk away? Why or why not? What are some other healthy boundary-setting strategies? Can you think of any examples where walking away may not be the best solution?

8. Set Realistic Expectations for Relationships

It can be difficult to set healthy boundaries with family members, especially if you have a history of unhealthy relationships. However, it is possible to set realistic expectations for relationships and challenge your reader to devise solutions for dealing with a few possible scenarios. In this chapter, we will discuss one way to set healthy boundaries with family members and provide a few examples. We will also assess your knowledge so far by asking several questions.

Setting realistic expectations for relationships is crucial when setting healthy boundaries. For example, if you have a history of being treated poorly by family members, you may expect them to continue that behavior. However, by setting realistic expectations, you can challenge yourself to change the way you interact with them. You may need to set some rules or limits in order to do so, but it is important to remember that you are worth protecting. It is also important to remember that not all family members are the same and that some may be willing to change their behavior if given a chance.

One way to set realistic expectations for relationships is to come up with solutions for dealing with a few possible scenarios. For example, what would you do if a family member treated you poorly? Would you confront them or try to ignore them? What if they refused to change their behavior? How would you handle that? It is important to think about these things in advance so that you can be prepared when they happen.

9. Talk It Out

One way to set healthy boundaries with family members is to talk it out. Sit down with the person who you feel is crossing your boundaries and explain how you feel. Be assertive, but also be respectful. It's important to remember that you're both adults, and you're both entitled to your own opinions and feelings. If the conversation gets heated, try to take a step back and take a deep breath. Remember that the goal here is to come up with a solution that works for both of you - rather than starting a fight.

Once you've talked about your boundary issues, try to come up with some solutions together. Perhaps there are certain times when it's okay for the person to borrow your car, or maybe you can agree on an amount of money that they can borrow from you. Whatever the solution is, it's important that both of you are on board. If someone isn't respecting your boundary - even if it was agreed upon - then it's time to have another talk.

It can be difficult to set boundaries with family members, but it's important to do what's best for you. By talking things out and being assertive, you can establish healthy boundaries which will benefit both of you in the long run.

Chapter 6: How to Immediately Improve Your Child's Behavior

Children often mimic the behaviors they observe, whether from you, other adults in their lives, or the media they consume. As long as you consistently guide your child in the appropriate way to behave, whether by instructing them, setting an example for them, correcting them, or using any other method, your child will eventually internalize the appropriate behavior.

There are a few tips that you can use to your advantage to set healthy boundaries for your children.
https://pixabay.com/es/photos/adulto-madre-hija-playa-ni%c3%b1os-1807500/

Your child's behavior will improve more rapidly if you praise them for their good manners rather than simply criticizing and punishing them when they test your patience. This chapter will focus on what you can do to improve your child's behavior, including setting limits and knowing what to avoid in specific situations.

You will learn how to set boundaries and improve your child's habits, and we will also take you on a practical journey, explaining common-case scenarios involving children and how you can positively influence their behavior.

How to Positively Influence Your Child's Behavior

The manner in which your child behaves can reveal a great deal about your attitude and personality and whether or not your child is being raised in a suitable environment.

The following are some positive ways you can influence your child's behavior:

Express Your Feelings

Communication is essential in all aspects of relationships. Whenever your child does something, whether indoors or outdoors, good or bad, be sure to let them know how you feel about it. If you disregard your emotions, your kids will do anything without considering, "What will my parents say?"

Children often say, "My dad said..." or, "My mom told me...." When you tell them something, ask them to repeat it to make sure they heard you, and tell them it makes you happy when they do so.

Communicate directly with them by using "I" or the name they call you to put them in your shoes and enable them to see things from your point of view. For example, "I don't like how you whined when I said "No" today after explaining the reason why," or, "Mom will be angry if you remove your shoes," or, "Do you think it makes dad happy when you argue?"

Set Good Examples

Your child will probably imitate your behavior more closely than you think. You should set an example for them in the way that you communicate with them and in the way that you interact with other people.

Everything you do wrong, no matter how trivial you think it is, sends a message to your child about how they should behave in a given situation. Most children enjoy bragging to their friends and classmates about what goes on in their homes and will act accordingly when playing. However, they are unaware of whether or not this will leave a favorable impression.

Do not simply correct and instruct them and then walk away. Your child will emulate the good examples you set by following your lead.

For example, use the magic words "please," "excuse me," "sorry," "thank you," and "pardon me" in all necessary situations, and you'll find your child doing the same. By incorporating it into a song as a constant reminder, you help them remember it better.

If you do not want your child to be rude and controlling, refrain from doing so yourself, especially in their presence, and always speak politely. Always correct them when they are out of line, and they will readily comply because they will observe you doing the same. Otherwise, they will call you out for your behavior.

Appreciate Their Efforts

Children crave attention and will likely do anything to obtain it. If they are not getting your attention when they do the right thing, they may try doing the wrong thing to see how you react, and they will almost certainly get your attention then. To mitigate this, acknowledge their efforts to impress you, even if it's a routine act of kindness.

When your child follows your rules, respond positively. For example, you could say, *"I really appreciate you doing the laundry before my return. You're the best."* When they have unintentionally done something that displeases you, call them out, but don't leave them hanging.

If they shattered a plate while washing it, instead of saying, *"Don't you pay attention to anything you do?"* it is preferable to ask, *"Did it hurt you? Please be extra careful next time, okay?"* or *"You make things easier for me by doing the dishes, but please do it carefully."*

They will gladly accept correction when you say, *"I've noticed that you always clean up after yourself. Well done,"* and when they forget, you can say, *"I'm glad you always clean up after yourself. I think this is a good habit to continue."*

When you do not praise them and then ask, *"Why didn't you clean up after yourself?"* they may not respond and clean up anyway, or they may say, *"I've always done it. You just don't notice."*

Be Firm

Be certain of your words before speaking to them. Perhaps you were certain but have since changed your mind. Inform your child immediately and explain why. Always keep your word, and avoid making promises you cannot fulfill.

Clarify your speech by allowing your yes to mean yes and your no to mean no. When you don't go back on your word or bend a strict rule, you teach your child that you mean what you say. Say no if you know it will benefit everyone. Try to always tell them the truth and not justify a lie with "I was only joking" when the truth eventually comes out.

If you have stated something clearly and your child appears to be disregarding it, ask them directly, "What did I say about this?" (This should not be a rhetorical question). For instance, you may tell your child to put down their phone and come and assist you, stating that if you have to call them again, you'll temporarily confiscate their phone.

If you eventually call them again, don't make it a bluff. Take action immediately. Give them constructive criticism in a loving manner. Always reinforce your rules and remind them of the consequences if they break them.

Allow Disappointment

No one is perfect, least of all a child. Children are naturally prone to making mistakes. They are naive and easily influenced, and they can sometimes lose track of who they are. Be cautious and patient with them, and encourage them constantly as they make gradual progress in their learning.

How do you react if your child eats food from a stranger or begs from other kids? When they are being stubborn, you can have a calm conversation with them or give them a mild rebuke, but you should never abuse or ridicule them. This irritates them. Disappointment can strike at any time, and you may feel compelled to teach your kids a life lesson, forgetting that they are still developing and require time to adapt.

Try your best to make them happy by providing the essentials they need to prevent them from engaging in this behavior and explain why they cannot have certain things. Assure them that you are their parent and that they should not be afraid to ask you for anything. However, you should not guarantee that you'll always provide it for them.

Teach them to be satisfied with what they have and recognize that not everything they desire is necessary.

Allow Them the Freedom of Expression

You must make space for your child to speak to you while demonstrating that you are paying attention to what they are saying. Follow up and participate in their conversations by speculating what will happen next.

For example, when they are describing their school experience, and they reach the part that requires them to ask their teacher for permission, respond with how you anticipated them to have behaved, and they will take note.

Allow your child the freedom to express themselves.
https://unsplash.com/photos/YLMs82LF6FY

You can say something like, *"Let me guess, you politely raised your hand and said, "Please excuse me, ma'am,"* while smiling. If they laugh it off or say, *"No, mom, I just raised my hand and was excused,"* you can say something like, *"The next time you want to go, it's better to be politely specific about what you want to do, okay?"*

Make certain you receive a response from them. This fosters an atmosphere where they feel safe to share their thoughts and feelings while also being open to new ideas and suggestions.

It demonstrates that you are willing to listen to them, respect them, and make them feel at ease. They may feel better after venting to you about their problems.

Establish a Close Bond

When you create an environment in which your children feel totally comfortable around you and are able to open up to you about anything that is bothering them or going on in their lives, it is extremely simple to influence their behavior.

When asked who their best friends are, some children name one or both of their parents. They will always do whatever it takes to maintain your satisfaction with them.

As a close bond is formed between you and them, you'll be able to easily tune into their emotions, participate in every decision they make, and influence their thoughts. They will want to know the things you approve of and disapprove of.

Don't alienate them by constantly making fun of them. They are offended when you say things like that, even if they do not speak up to avoid being rude or hurting your feelings.

You don't have to make them observe you improve their behavior because they'll do things with you in mind if you have their attention. Some children will say, "Wait until I tell my mom what you did," or "I will definitely tell my dad what you did."

Curtail Your Relationships

The friends and people you surround yourself with will shape your character and how you interact with others, including your child. Your children can learn from and imitate your friends, with or without your knowledge.

Teach them the importance of maintaining a positive social circle and surrounding themselves with productive influences. Ensure that they have suitable play dates and take them to appropriate gatherings.

Inform them that saying "I'm sorry" goes a long way and that prioritizing relationships is more important than being right. Tell them that it is their responsibility to maintain healthy relationships at all times, not through coercion but through openness and honesty.

Set Your Boundaries

The simplest way to establish boundaries is to make "family rules" that everyone must follow. Clarify and simplify your instructions so there is no excuse for not following them. You must make your children accountable for their actions by issuing a warning for the first infraction, detailing the consequences for a second offense, and getting them to agree with you.

For instance, you can give them a specific amount of money for a given timeframe with the promise that you'll increase it if they actually keep it for that period. When they fulfill your request, honor your word, and increase the amount of money. However, if they fail to do so, they must complete the period without additional compensation.

When you do this, your child will learn to trust and respect you. They know better than to try to get you to change your mind because of supposed consequences, and they know you won't let them down when you say something reassuring.

Reasons Why Boundaries Should Be Managed

Although giving a child the same rights as an adult is not appropriate, some parents put their child's feelings before their own. Most parents allow their children to use their emotions to get what they want rather than setting limits on their behavior.

Some of the reasons why setting boundaries in a family is important are listed below:

Limiting Rights and Narcissism

Due to their love for their children, parents sometimes allow their children's desires and emotions to trump their instructions. Setting limits does not indicate that you love them any less but rather that you want them to develop maturity and patience by understanding that the world does not revolve around them.

They will be less likely to develop narcissistic tendencies and will be more equipped to handle life's inevitable challenges if they grow up with the assurance that their parents will enforce reasonable limits on their freedom and independence.

By establishing limits, your child may learn to feel compassion for those who are less fortunate.

Setting Boundaries as a Learning Platform

We can only get better at things by attempting new things and mastering the ones we've already learned. It is a positive and healthy thought for parents to consider that their child will require adaptable skills to succeed in the world.

Instilling in children the knowledge that they will, at some point, be responsible for themselves is important. This will help them prepare for the future and make it easier for themselves.

They should also be aware that their parents will not always be available to solve their problems and alleviate their difficulties, so they must learn to adapt to changing circumstances.

Setting Boundaries to Feel Secure

Regardless of the boundaries that are established, you should leave room for negotiation with your children. Otherwise, they will be ineffective. Routines and family rules, such as bedtime, screen time, shared chores, mealtime, etc., will reduce your child's doubts and obsessions.

Even as your children express their emotions, you should not trade them for their safety. Setting boundaries does not imply that you are a mean parent, even if your child may accuse you of being unfair at times for sticking to them.

Being a parent should be a sufficient reason to establish boundaries, which should be done calmly but firmly to promote your child's sense of security and safety.

Protection from Physical and Mental Harm

Our primary obligation as parents is to protect our children from any harm, whether physical or emotional. Boundaries are set for protection, not to control people. Explain the rationale behind the boundaries you set for better clarity.

Exclusion causes emotional abuse in children. Set boundaries early to avoid damage, especially from misunderstanding. Boundaries will help your children to know when to do things.

Parenting Boundaries

There are indicators of how well your boundaries are established when grooming a child. Most children appreciate positive instructions over negative ones because it encourages them to think positively. The following are necessary boundaries that you can implement in your home:

- Not doing things for your kids that they are capable of doing themselves.
- Not letting your child's temporary mood ruin your happiness.
- Not treating your child's life as yours by being in complete control.
- Not constantly putting your child in the spotlight.
- Not giving your child complete control over your home.

How to Set Healthy Boundaries

You can use the following tips when setting boundaries to make sure you're not too hard on your child and to ensure you're doing what is best for them. Among them are the following:

- Don't be overly emphatic with your child.
- Know why you need to set a boundary.
- Talk it and walk it.
- Take charge of yourself.
- Respect your boundaries and those of others.
- Communicate consequences for crossing boundaries.
- Express yourself.
- Let the impact of the boundary be felt.
- Don't stress yourself.
- Be assertive without feeling guilty.
- Be confident in saying "no."

Tricky Scenarios

How do you react when your boundaries are violated, and what do you do about it? Consider the following case studies:

- Your children interrupt your conversation with other adults without trying to catch your attention or politely excuse themselves.

- You're in a shopping mall, and your children keep nagging you to get them a toy. You eventually say "No," and they begin to cry.
- You get home from work, and your children haven't done the dishes or their homework. You scold them, and they get nasty.

Questions

- What do you do with all the emotions you may be experiencing, such as embarrassment about what others may think of your child's attitude?
- Are you going to discipline them in that case?
- Will you get them the toy? What will you say to get them to stop?
- Will you be able to control your rage toward them and persuade them to do your bidding without emotionally harming them?

As a means of enhancing your child's behavior, it is crucial to establish limits so that they do not harbor pent-up emotions that, when released, can cause chaos. It's your guilt-free way of saying "Yes" to yourself and "No" to your child whenever it's in your best interest.

It's a method of teaching your child appropriate behavior. When you understand your role and status in your family and your child's life, you'll know what you are expected to do and what you should not take from your child.

Chapter 7: 7 Psychological Tricks to Deal with Negative Friends

In today's world, it is natural to be exposed to many negative things or circumstances. But how do you deal with negative friends? And how can you stop them from making you feel bad? The answer is, of course, setting boundaries. Everyone is prone to negativity and how we respond to it determines how much of an impact it has on our lives. Here we will discuss what a negative friend looks like and how to stay calm when dealing with them so that it doesn't adversely affect your life.

Setting boundaries with your friends strengthens your bond.
https://unsplash.com/photos/Cecb0_8Hx-o

Boundaries with Friends Are Different

Boundaries with friends are different from those with family members. When you have a close relationship with someone, the lines can be blurry between what is acceptable and what is not. Family ties are generally more unconditional, and friends come and go.

If a friend asks you to do something that goes against your values or beliefs, it can be easy to get caught up in their request without thinking it through first. But when it comes to family members, there are clear lines of respect and trust that aren't as blurred. People who are close to you may know when you're upset and could try to help you work through your emotions. But friends may want to help you out instead of listening to what you have to say. They might not take your feelings seriously, which can lead to confusion and frustration on both sides and can cause tension. You should always make sure that the boundaries between you and your friends are clear in your head before any requests are made so that misunderstandings don't arise later on! And if they're negative friends, the need for boundaries is even more essential.

Is Your Friend Negative?

We've all been there before. A friend we thought was a good friend turns out to be toxic, leaving us wondering why. How can someone we were so trusting of turn out to be the exact opposite? It can leave you feeling disappointed and hurt - but how do you know if they're actually a bad friend or just negative?

Some friends come with baggage, while other friends are toxic to your growth. Here are some of the types of negative friends you need to create boundaries with.

The Jealous Friend

Jealousy is a common emotion that can occur in any type of relationship. A jealousy-prone person could be someone who has a close relationship with another person and feels jealous when they see them become more successful or happier than they are. If your friend is jealous of your success or envies the path that your career has taken, then you have a toxic friend on your hands. Jealousy is a very nasty thing to deal with, especially when it comes from someone you thought was a friend. If your friend is always talking about how much better your achievements are than theirs, that's a sign that there's something that's really bothering them.

The Overly Critical Friend

An overly critical friend is one who constantly finds things wrong with you and your behavior, no matter how big or small. They can get annoyed by how messy you are or how slow you are to get ready in the morning. Even if you haven't done anything wrong, they will always have an opinion about something you have done. Oftentimes, they are just looking for attention from people around them and may not even realize it. An overly critical friend can be an emotional burden on anyone who has to deal with them on a daily basis. They can take up a lot of your time and energy just by constantly criticizing you. As a result, they can make it feel like you are never good enough at anything. This can lead to anxiety and low self-esteem when everything you do is questioned.

The Self-Involved Friend

Some people are naturally more talkative than others, but if your friend only ever talks about themselves, it can be hard to stay engaged in the conversation. Having a one-sided conversation where you're just sitting and smiling as your friend talks about their latest vacation or promotion can be frustrating and tiring. A self-involved friend is one who acts only for their own interest and does not genuinely care about the wellbeing of others. Self-involved friends know what they want and are more focused on taking care of themselves than others. They can be a real drag on relationships because they don't put in the effort to help others, and they don't take much responsibility for their actions. Self-involved friends are likely to brag, blame others, and make excuses for their actions. They are more likely to be selfish, judgmental, and have unrealistic expectations. They also tend to be shallower than other people.

The Lying Friend

A friend who often lies always tells you half-truths, even when they know you don't want to hear them. They may make promises they can't keep or go back on their word after you have trusted them. They may also make up stories about things that never happened in order to get you to do or think what they want you to do or think. A friend who lies often is not someone you can trust. If it turns out that they are lying to you, it could ruin your trust in everyone else as well. Lying like this is usually a sign of insecurities. So, while it can be annoying, they might also be a really great friend to you.

The Overstepping Friend

An overstepping friend is someone who constantly interferes with your life. They take advantage of your generosity, your kindness, and your emotional state. Overstepping friends are opportunists who use you for their own benefit. They might want something from you but may not be likely to give anything in return. Or they could just want to get close to you. They may not intend to harm you, but they will be more interested in having their way than in helping you achieve your goals and ambitions. This causes you to lose focus and get sidetracked because they are always trying to take over the situation. When they take over, they usually do so in a destructive way, which can lead to feelings of frustration, anger, and resentment. This can cause problems for both of you. On the one hand, it makes your friendship difficult and strained. On the other hand, it can leave you open to exploitation or other types of abuse.

The Attention-Seeking Friend

Attention-seeking friends are those who are constantly looking for ways to get noticed by their friends and family. They'll often get negative and over-exaggerate about a funny situation or joke just to be noticed. There's nothing wrong with wanting people to notice you, but if a friend is constantly complaining about things and constantly trying to get your attention, it can be quite annoying. Attention-seeking friends will also often have a reputation for being unreliable and use their attention-seeking behavior in many different ways, including asking people for help, seeking advice, or crying.

Friendship is a beautiful thing, and it can be so powerful when done correctly. However, it can also be a negative thing when you have toxic friends in your life. It's important to recognize these negative friends and either confront them or distance yourself from them. Only then can you be sure that you're surrounding yourself with positive people who are actually worthy of being called a "friend." There is no easy way out of dealing with an overly critical friend, but there are some things you can do to cope with the situation. Boundaries!

7 Psychological Tricks to Deal with Negative Friends

If you find that you have negative friends in your life, it's not the end of the world. You may not be able to change their attitude, but there are some psychological tricks you can use to help you to deal with them.

1. Be Kind

Psychologists have determined that the human brain is more inclined toward seeing the negative aspect of life. We are hardwired to fixate on the threat. They call this the negativity bias. Negativity bias is the tendency for humans to pay more attention to negative experiences than positive ones. It can have a profound impact on human behavior, especially in social situations. In regard to your friend, you can either choose to see the world through pessimistic eyes or optimistic ones. Negativity can be draining and annoying, but if you have the patience, kindness, and willingness to help that person see a brighter side of life, it will go a long way. If somebody is being negative toward you, it means that they see something in you that they don't like. So what? You can choose to be offended or use it as an opportunity to show them their negativity is unfounded. People are critical because their view of the world has been conditioned by their past experiences, traumas, and insecurities. It isn't personal but rather a reflection of them as people. Try asking questions instead of making excuses and defending yourself when someone says something hurtful or negative about you. Listen without judgment and understand where they are coming from before responding with your own opinion. Negative people appreciate those who are kinder than them and who lift them up instead of breaking them down further into darkness.

2. Respond Calmly

When people are negative around you, it can be hard to know how to respond. If someone is being rude or condescending, it's natural to want to lash back in a way that feels like a challenge. But if you respond in kind, you might lose your temper and worsen the situation. The last thing you want to do is add fuel to the fire by engaging in a heated argument with your friend. Instead, try to remain calm and focus on what your friend is saying. Once you understand what's going on, you can decide how best to respond. When it comes to negative friends, there are a few different things that you can do. Be sure to use polite and respectful words, no matter how upset you feel.

- First, you can try to talk with them about why they're feeling the way they are. This will allow you to better understand each other and hopefully bring about some positive change.

- Second, you can try to find ways in which you can help your friend. Perhaps by offering words of encouragement or simply listening to them when they need support.
- Finally, you can take it upon yourself to be more positive and supportive yourself. By doing this, you will not only help yourself feel better but also have an impact on your friend as well.

You can also try putting yourself in the other person's shoes before responding. Imagine how your response would make them feel if they were in your shoes. This can help you evaluate your response more objectively and can even help you change your original reaction. By taking a step back and thinking about the other person's perspective, you can avoid escalating an argument that could have been avoided in the first place. Don't feed their negativity by arguing back or agreeing with everything they say. Because no matter how much you argue, they are not going to change. Instead, just continue living your life the way you want to.

3. Don't Argue with Them

Don't get into an argument with a negative friend. If you do, your friend will undoubtedly become more negative and aggressive in their disposition towards you. This is because they will be trying to "prove" themselves and show that they are right by pushing back against what you say or do to make you look bad.

It doesn't matter if you are right or wrong. It is better to just let the conversation go and not engage with negativity. This way, your friend will remain quiet and not contribute to the negativity in your life. You can always talk to them later when they are feeling more positive. If you do choose to engage with your negative friend, try to stay calm and focused on what you want to discuss instead of getting upset yourself. This is especially useful if your friend is feeling stressed or under pressure. And if the person is having a bad day and raising their voice, just take a deep breath and let them calm down before responding. Or try to help them find ways to relax, like going to a movie or having a drink.

4. Avoid Their Triggers

Maybe you have a friend who hates their job, and they begin to get extremely negative whenever it comes up in conversation. Maybe they are really into politics and get into the negative aspects of life whenever the subject comes up. Or maybe they have a very negative view of themselves and get self-critical. By sticking to light topics when you're hanging out with a negative friend, you can avoid feeling like you're on the defensive. You can steer the conversation toward something that makes you happy or something you both enjoy discussing. If they are bringing up topics that don't interest you, just have a chat about something else. Of course, this may mean missing out on opportunities for bonding, but in the long run, it will be worth it. Another way to deal with a negative friend during a conversation is to take what they are saying with a grain of salt. No matter how true their words seem, if they are being negative, they are probably exaggerating things. If they seem to be stuck in a perpetual state of negativity, try to take breaks from them so that you can have some more positive conversations. And last but not least, try not to get too personal and avoid topics that can be upsetting if they're going through a tough time.

5. Empathize with Them

It can be really hard to empathize when a negative friend is having a bad day or struggling with a particular situation. Negative friends are often draining and frustrating, but witnessing their pain can also be really painful. As a result, it can be hard for us to understand what they're going through. Empathizing with a friend can help them better understand your feelings and hopefully change their behavior. Empathizing is the process of understanding another person's feelings, perspectives, or situations by relating or sharing your own feelings and emotions. It can be done in many ways depending on the relationship you have with your friend.

It is important to understand that a negative friend's behavior is largely influenced by their upbringing and past experiences. Knowing how the negative friend grew up or what events have occurred in their lives can help you better empathize with them in general. For example, if the negative friend was bullied as a child, you can try to understand how they feel when others make fun of them. You should also empathize if you see yourself in the person you're empathizing with or share similar values or beliefs, making it easier for you to understand where they're coming from. For example, if you are close friends with someone who is struggling with depression, you may be more likely to empathize with them because of the shared experience. Similarly, if the negative friend has had challenges in relationships, you can try to imagine how it feels to be *them* in these situations. By empathizing with a negative friend on an emotional level, you can help to change their behavior and improve your relationship with them. You may also be able to help your friend see that their actions do matter and that they don't need to be so hard on themselves in order to change their behavior.

6. Be Responsible for Your Reaction

It can be easy to react negatively to a friend, especially when the relationship has been rocky. To avoid reacting in a negative way, it is best to take a step back and observe your own behavior. When you take the time to analyze the situation, you are less likely to get angry or upset. Furthermore, you are better equipped to deal with issues that arise by taking the time to understand how you feel and why you can make smarter decisions.

- First, if you are feeling overwhelmed by the situation, you should take time to calm down and plan how you'll respond. If it is possible, it may be best to spend time alone so that you can think about how to approach the situation from the best angle.
- It is also important not to let yourself get dragged into an argument with your friend. Remember that this is your friend, and they may just be having a bad day. Try to empathize and remember that everyone has good days and bad days.

Finally, remember that everyone makes mistakes and has moments of weakness. You should not judge them for these moments but rather accept them as part of who they are.

7. Ignore Their Comments

A negative friend can be a drag on your day, and it's even harder if you spend a lot of time with that person. There's no reason to get upset when a friend has a negative opinion. If you feel like a friend is being mean to you, ignore them. Don't respond, and just move on with your day. They'll probably get the message and stop bothering you about it.

With all of that being said, there are times when it's best to respond to negative comments with kindness and positivity. If someone is speaking negatively about you and others, you need to stand up for yourself and others who are affected by their words. First and foremost, remember that everyone is entitled to their opinion. Don't take things personally, and try to figure out what the person is trying to say. If you feel like you need to respond, make sure that you're always respectful. You don't want to come off as angry or defensive. Your goal is to be positive and kind, and that will show in your interactions with others. No matter how uncomfortable this will feel, you need to show that person that their opinions don't match the facts — and that they should stop spreading false information. If this doesn't work, it may be time to take a break or even end the friendship.

Negative Friend Scenarios and Fixes

Remember that having a negative attitude can be contagious. If you are not careful around your negative friend, you'll get sucked into their way of thinking. Without using the above boundaries, you'll turn into that very person that bothered you in the first place.

Take a moment to think about it. If any of the following are true for you, then you need to start thinking of ways to deal with your negative friend.

    1. Do you find it difficult to calm down after meeting with them?

    YES/NO

    Yes? Then limit how much time you spend with them. Or, if things begin to get negative, make an excuse to leave.

    2. When you think of seeing them, do you experience strong levels of discomfort?

    YES/NO

    Yes? Then consider not picking up the phone when they call or delaying your response if they text you.

    3. When you're around them, do you behave in ways that go against your values?

    YES/NO

    Yes? Try steering any negative inducing conversations away from things you know they'll complain about.

    4. Have you tried to talk to them about their negative behavior?

    YES/NO

    Yes? Take the time to put yourself first. If they refuse to change, then the next step is up to you.

    No? Then use the tips in this book to approach your friend with an open and honest attitude and explain to them exactly what is bothering you. They may not even know they are being negative until someone tells them.

If you have a hard time dealing with a friend who's constantly negative, or if you're being negative, it can be tempting to turn to sarcasm and harsh comments to make someone else feel bad. But doing so only feeds into their negativity and makes your situation worse. Instead, try talking to them about it and listen to what they have to say. This will help strengthen your bond with them and even help change their mindset. And if they don't start becoming positive, don't stop being positive yourself! If a friend is being negative all the time, this could mean that they are experiencing some kind of personal problem that you can help them work through together. Be patient with them, and keep in mind that there's always a way out of any situation.

Chapter 8: How to Get That Promotion without People Pleasing

Many people fall into the trap of saying "Yes" to everything, even if it means they have to jeopardize their own happiness and wellbeing. They try to do everything to ensure that they're well-liked among their peers and bosses. Unfortunately, many people think that being a people-pleaser is the only way to get a promotion and climb up the ranks.

Upon reading this chapter, you'll learn how people-pleasing can harm your professional career and how it won't help you get a promotion. You will come across a step-by-step guide on how to stop being highly accommodating, as well as how to boost your self-confidence and reinforce your boundaries in the process. Finally, you'll find a self-assessment that will help you determine if you're a people-pleaser, along with some scenarios and their solutions.

Learning how to get ahead at work without people-pleasing is a crucial skill to have.
https://unsplash.com/photos/eF7HN40WbAQ

Why People-Pleasing Can Harm Your Professional Career

There are many people who please and expect to be pleased in a professional setting, which is why it can often seem like the best way to get things done and get ahead at work. We are all naturally inclined to do things for people and maybe even suck up to them to get them to like us. However, what we don't realize is that this habit can backfire in a work (and non-work) environment.

In the process of trying to please others, you ultimately lose sight of yourself. You get consumed by their wants and needs and aim to satisfy them even if it means compromising your own happiness. There will always be a part of you that realizes that you can't force someone to like you, which is why you feel the need to do more. If your boss has bad intentions, they'll likely exploit you and overload you without the intention of rewarding you for your hard work. Eventually, you'll fall completely out of touch with yourself and your sense of direction.

People-pleasers typically compare themselves to others. They're seldom satisfied with their accomplishments because they tear themselves apart when they see that their peers have accomplished more. You convince yourself that you're smaller than your co-workers (the inferiority complex), which reinforces the people-pleasing cycle and takes you further away from your goals.

Being a people-pleaser prompts you to say "yes" to everything that people ask you to do. This can be quite burdensome and overwhelming and may affect your ability to complete your work. You are left with very little room for self-improvement and even self-care.

Besides the mental and physical effects of being a yes-person, being a people-pleaser can leave you with a negative sense of self. You realize that many people in your life are walking all over you, and yet you can't bring yourself to say "No" to their requests. This can make you feel weak and inadequate.

Why People-Pleasers Don't Get Promoted

Being a people-pleaser can ensure that you're well-liked among your peers and manager. However, it will not get you far when it comes to climbing up the ranks. When considering candidates for leadership positions, there is much more to consider, such as respect, reliability, and assertiveness.

Everyone loves having a co-worker who is willing to help pick up the slack without complaining. You're ready to do the work that no one else is willing to do, and while that earns you points for likeability, it doesn't count for anything in terms of respect. If there are specific tasks that no one likes doing, chances are you don't either. However, volunteering or even agreeing to take these tasks on in addition to your own responsibilities can make you come across as a pushover. Leadership roles require you to delegate tasks and ensure that everyone gets their job done.

If you're not assertive, your team members will protest whenever they get assigned tasks they don't wish to do and will either try to get you to reassign them or find a co-worker who is willing to please and take on these tasks. As a leader, you won't have the time to shift things around to please everyone or do the tasks that no one wishes to do. If you manage to do that, your team members will take it for granted and view it as an opportunity to slack off at work. In other words, they won't respect you as a leader. Assigning all the undesirable tasks to the one person who is willing to do all the work isn't a solution either. Overburdening an employee is not a sign of good leadership and will likely decrease the efficiency of your function or department at work.

Overly-accommodating individuals often have a fear of making mistakes. Even though they willingly bite off more than they can chew, they spend more time on tasks than they're supposed to. They're terrified of making mistakes, which can make them obsessive about producing quality work. Other people don't understand this, which is why they think people-pleasers can't multitask and handle several responsibilities. You may notice that some of your peers do less than you and don't have the same attention to detail, but you still manage to get ahead. While producing quality work is important, being very nit-picky can hold you back and mess with your time management efforts. There are very limited workday hours, and you must be mindful of how you spend them.

People-pleasers don't respond well to criticism, even if it's constructive. They take it as a sign of disapproval, which causes them to second-guess their abilities. Valid negative feedback must be accepted and learned from so that a person can grow and develop. If people notice that criticism affects you more than it should, they'll take you for someone who's fragile and will treat you in this way. They'll withhold constructive comments from you even if you need them, and therefore, they won't be able to trust you to take on more responsibilities.

If you have a fear of disapproval, you'll find it hard to be disagreeable, even if the situation calls for it. You won't take action if anyone crosses your boundaries or disrespects you, which gives people the impression that they can easily take advantage of you. Since you don't want to be disagreeable, you'll likely shy away from voicing your opinions. This allows others to judge you as someone who doesn't have convictions and can't make decisions, which assures them that you aren't cut out for a leadership role.

Someone with a fear of disapproval may shy away from giving negative feedback and calling out unacceptable behaviors. They may also feel reluctant to make unpopular decisions, which is something that managers often have to do.

How to Stop People-Pleasing

Helping others out and doing nice things for them is something that we should all aspire to do. However, we should know to stop when it comes at the expense of our own comfort, self-expression, feelings, respect, boundaries, and success. Fortunately, there are some things you can do to stop being a people-pleaser and grow your confidence, happiness, and productivity in the process.

Step 1: Grow Your Sense of Self-Awareness

Any personal changes require you to grow your sense of self-awareness. You must track how often you express people-pleasing tendencies, such as saying "Yes" to things you don't want to do. Write these instances down and then reflect on what you could have done instead. Doing this will teach you how to handle situations more effectively in the future.

Step 2: Set Clear Boundaries

Growing your awareness can make it easier to identify your boundaries and how you allow others to overstep them. Write down your limitations in a journal and recount how it feels whenever someone disregards them. This will encourage you to communicate your boundaries to others and take action whenever someone transgresses them.

Step 3: Reach Out for Support

Being a people-pleaser can be very difficult to overcome. You need to learn how to be comfortable with putting your needs above the needs of others and accept that not everyone is going to like you. This is why having a supportive friend, mentor, family member, or even co-worker by your side can be invaluable. Ask them to help you develop an action plan and stay on track.

Step 4: Take Baby Steps

You'll find it really hard to start turning down everyone's requests all of a sudden. Even if you have a rich personality, you may have always identified as being a nice and likable person. Doing things that may influence the way others think of you and how you perceive yourself can give rise to an identity crisis.

It takes time to get used to the idea of saying "No," but you need to remind yourself that it will get easier over time. You'll find that the sense of fulfillment you used to obtain from being agreeable is replaced by the satisfaction of doing what's best for you. Start by saying "no" using a text, as it's likely to be easier for you than having to do it face-to-face. You can also rehearse adaptable responses, such as "I'd love to help, but I have a lot on my plate at the moment," or "I'm sure that someone else would be better for that task than me."

Step 5: Set Realistic Goals

You may feel compelled to change your entire personality overnight. However, you need to remember that dramatic changes aren't sustainable. You've been a people-pleaser for as long as you can remember, so it doesn't make sense to throw away a large part of who you are all of a sudden. Make sure to set yourself realistic goals, such as turning down a co-worker's request for help on a project (if you know that they don't need it or if you'll end up doing the entire task on your own) every other week. In meetings, try to speak up and express your opinion, even when it's different from everyone else's.

Step 6: Seek Help

Asking other people for help can go against your nature of being the person that people always come to for help. You need to recognize that asking for help every now and then isn't a sign of weakness. Start asking people to help you out, even if they're going to assist you with minor tasks.

Step 7: Avoid Self-Deprecating Talk

You need to stop tying your entire sense of self-worth to the work you do, your likeability, and your ability to please others. The first step you need to do is to stop engaging in self-deprecating talk and change the feelings you have toward yourself. Reciting affirmations can feel awkward at first. However, you'll find that it's a great way to boost your confidence.

Here are some ideas for self-affirming mantras that you can use:

"I am true to myself. I won't attempt to please others."

"I say "No" to whatever doesn't feel right for me. I'm not responsible for other people's happiness."

"I am only responsible for my feelings."

Step 8: Take a Moment Before You Respond

Saying "Yes" comes naturally to you, which is why you always agree to things that you regret later. Make it a habit to pause for a moment before you respond to other people's requests. Don't hesitate to tell them that you need to check your calendar before you give them an answer.

Step 9: Lose the Excuses

Remember that you don't need an excuse to turn down a person's request. Besides the fact that they will likely adjust their wording to convince you to do whatever they want, you have the right to say "No" to something simply because you don't wish to do it.

Step 10: Stay True to Yourself

Most importantly, you should never compromise your values, convictions, and comfort to please someone else. Sticking to whatever you believe is right *for you* earns the respect of others and yourself.

Self-Assessment: Are You a People-Pleaser?

Here's a quick self-assessment that can help you determine if you're a people pleaser:

- People often take advantage of your kindness.
- You feel resentful because people don't appreciate the fact that you spend all of your time doing things for them.
- You give more than you receive in your relationships.
- Your co-workers aren't there to help you, but they always come to you whenever they need help.
- You bite off more than you can chew, which leaves you feeling stressed and burned out.
- You always apologize even when you've done nothing wrong.
- Your friends and family are frustrated with you because you spend all of your time working.
- You agree with everything others say even when you really don't.
- You struggle to say "No" or turn others down.
- You're not true to yourself around others.
- Criticism can make you doubt your overall abilities.
- You have a negative sense of self and low self-esteem.
- The thought of angering someone scares you.
- You find it hard to be true to yourself around others.
- You need everyone to like you.

People-Pleaser Scenarios and Solutions

1. Your co-worker needs to submit a project by the end of the day that they haven't started working on yet. They ask you to help them out, but you already have your own tasks to work on. Would you help them immediately?

    Yes / No

    If you said yes, your co-worker probably knew when their project was due beforehand and failed to manage their time effectively. You should explain that you have your own tasks to work on since you're likely operating on a tight schedule as well. You should only help them out if you have the time after you've finished with your own tasks.

2. You're at a meeting to discuss the release of a new product. Everyone thinks you should go ahead and release it now, but you think you should wait until Christmas when the sale volumes are high. Your boss is taking a final vote. Do you:

    Agree with everyone else / Tell them what you think

    If you would agree with everyone else, try to practice voicing your opinion even when it's different from everyone else's. You may be surprised at how often your ideas are taken into consideration. You shouldn't feel bad even if they aren't, as it doesn't make you any less competent.

3. Your boss comes up to you and says: "I noticed that you haven't been following the guidelines lately. Please read the guidelines before you start working on your projects to ensure that nothing is missing. I'd be happy to explain anything that you don't understand." Does their feedback make you doubt your abilities and competence?

    Yes / No

    If you said yes: you should remind yourself that everyone makes mistakes and that this doesn't make you any less competent or intelligent. You can't base your entire sense of self-worth on your work because it can be highly variable. You should trust in your abilities and maintain a high level of confidence regardless.

Now that you read this chapter, you are ready to express your authentic self and stop obsessing over the need to be liked by others. As you read the following chapter, you'll learn about common mistakes people make when they set boundaries and how to avoid making them.

Chapter 9: 10 Mistakes That May Make You Seem Fake

Self-improvement is a never-ending journey. Every day, we face new challenges and opportunities to grow as individuals. And while it's important to push ourselves out of our comfort zones, there's also value in setting boundaries and sticking to them. After all, personal boundaries help us define who we are and what we're comfortable with.

However, just as there's a fine line between self-improvement and self-care, there's also a fine line between healthy boundary-setting and overstepping our own boundaries. Oftentimes, we can be so focused on defining our personal limits that we end up putting ourselves at a disadvantage. For example, let's say you're an introvert who's working on being more social. In your quest to become more outgoing, you may start saying "yes" to every invitation you receive - even if that means constantly being exhausted and overwhelmed. Or maybe you've been dieting for months in an effort to lose weight, but you're so restrictive with your food choices that you're actually doing more harm than good. In both of these cases, the individual is so focused on expanding their boundaries that they forget to respect their own limits. As a result, they end up feeling burned out, resentful, and unhappy.

Setting boundaries will allow you to be your true self.
https://unsplash.com/photos/xpnRRH6z2NA

It can be scary setting and sticking to personal boundaries. After all, doing so requires us to be assertive, which can be a tough pill to swallow. However, it's important to remember that personal boundaries are there for a reason; to keep us healthy and safe physically and emotionally. With that in mind, here are four mistakes one could make when it comes to personal boundaries, along with some tips on how to avoid them.

Common Mistakes While Setting Self Boundaries

1. Prioritizing Everything

Everyone has their own set of boundaries, and when we stick to them, it helps us to feel safe and secure. However, there can be a downside to being too rigid about our boundaries. If we prioritize everything that falls within our boundaries, it can lead to us feeling overwhelmed and stressed. For example, let's say you have a strict rule about not working on weekends. However, you have a big project due on Monday morning. If you don't allow yourself to work on the project over the weekend, you may find yourself feeling anxious and stressed on Sunday night. In this case, it may be helpful to relax your boundaries slightly and allow yourself to work for a few hours on Saturday or Sunday. By doing so, you can minimize your stress levels and still stick to your boundary of not working excessive hours during the week.

Another possible mistake people make when sticking to their boundaries is being too inflexible. For example, let's say you have a rule that you'll never eat out at restaurants because you want to save money. However, if your friends invite you out to dinner and you refuse, they may eventually stop asking you to join them. As a result, you may miss out on social experiences and end up feeling isolated and lonely. In this case, it may be helpful to be more flexible with your boundaries and allow yourself to go out to dinner occasionally. Doing so can help you maintain social relationships and prevent you from feeling isolated.

Sticking to our boundaries is important, but we also need to be aware of the potential pitfalls of being too rigid or inflexible. By being mindful of these mistakes, we can ensure that our boundaries are helping us to feel safe and secure without leading to stress or isolation.

2. Over-functioning

A better approach is to set a boundary and then trust that people will respect it. You can handle the situation calmly and confidently without over-functioning if they don't.

It's important to stick to your boundaries, but it's also possible to over-function in an attempt to maintain them. Over-functioning can take many forms, but it generally refers to doing more than is necessary or appropriate in a given situation. For example, if you have a boundary that you don't allow others to cross, you may find yourself "over-functioning" by constantly monitoring the situation and intervening whenever someone comes close to breaking that boundary. This can be exhausting and ultimately counterproductive, as it can create resentment or build up a false sense of entitlement in those you're trying to protect your boundary with.

Over-functioning is a term that is used to describe a situation where someone takes on too much responsibility or tries to do too much for someone else. This can be a problem in any type of relationship, but it is particularly common in family relationships. Over-functioning can lead to feelings of resentment, anger, and exhaustion. It can also lead to problems in a relationship, such as conflict and diminished intimacy. There are a few key signs that you may be over-functioning in a relationship. First, do you find yourself always taking on more responsibility than the other person? Do you feel like you are always the one who has to put in more effort? Second, are you constantly doing things for the other person that they could easily do themselves? Are you always the one who has to initiate conversations or plans? Finally, do you feel like your needs are always last on the list? If you answered yes to any of these questions, then you may be over-functioning in your relationships. The good news is that there are ways to change this behavior. If you find yourself over-functioning, try to take a step back and allow the other person to take on more responsibility. Make sure you are taking care of yourself and making time for your needs. Lastly, communicate openly with the other person about your concerns. Taking these steps can help create a healthier balance in your relationships.

3. Dismissing Your Needs

When it comes to setting and maintaining personal boundaries, it's important to be mindful of your own needs. One common mistake people make is dismissing their own needs in favor of meeting the needs of others. This can leave you feeling resentful and taken for granted. It can also lead to burnout, as you're constantly giving without taking time to recharge. A healthy boundary-setting practice includes being honest about what you need to feel happy and fulfilled. If you find yourself constantly putting others' needs ahead of your own, it may be time to reassess your priorities. Remember, you deserve to nurture and care for yourself, too. By making your needs a priority, you can set a stronger foundation for healthy relationships with others.

We may convince ourselves that we don't have time for self-care or that we can't afford to nurture our own interests. However, this is not only unrealistic, but it is counterproductive. By neglecting our own needs, we're more likely to burn out and end up sacrificing our boundaries anyway. So instead of dismissing your needs, make sure to factor them into your decision-making process. At some point in our lives, we all face the challenge of sticking to our boundaries. Whether it's setting limits with our time, energy, or resources, it can be difficult to know where to draw the line. However, it's important to remember that our boundaries are there for a reason. They help us protect ourselves from being overwhelmed and taken advantage of.

4. Succumbing to FOMO

We've all been there before. You're out with your friends, having a great time, when suddenly someone starts talking about an event that you're not going to be able to attend. It could be a party, a concert, or even just a night out at a new restaurant. And as you listen to your friends discuss all the fun they're going to have without you, you start to feel a pang of regret. This feeling is known as FOMO, aka the Fear Of Missing Out.

One mistake people make when it comes to setting boundaries is succumbing to FOMO. With social media, we are constantly bombarded with images and stories of other people's seemingly perfect lives. We see our friends going on fun trips, taking fancy vacations, and experiencing all sorts of wonderful things, and we can't help but feel like we're missing out. Of course, we only see the highlights of other people's lives, so it's important to remember that comparison is the thief of joy. Just because someone else seems to be having a great time doesn't mean that you're not enjoying your own life.

Another way that FOMO can rear its ugly head is in our relationships. We may be afraid to set boundaries with our friends or family members because we don't want to miss out on time with them. However, it's important to remember that healthy relationships are built on trust and respect, and that includes respecting each other's boundaries. If you find yourself always saying "yes" to hanging out even when you really don't want to, it may be time to have a talk with your friend about setting some limits.

Ultimately, FOMO is a natural human emotion, but it's important not to let it dictate your life. If you find yourself falling into the trap of comparison or sacrificing your own needs for others, take a step back and reassess your priorities. Remember that you don't have to do everything or say "yes" to everything in order to have a fulfilling life.

5. Giving in to Fear

We all have self-boundaries: those lines we draw that indicate what we will and won't do, what we will and won't put up with, and what is and isn't acceptable to us. Most of the time, these boundaries serve us well. They help us to stay true to ourselves, protect us from harm, and keep our lives in line with our values. But there are times when these boundaries can trip us up. One mistake we often make is giving in to fear.

When we're afraid of something, it can be tempting to try to protect ourselves by retreating behind our self-boundaries. We may hide away from the world, refusing to step outside our comfort zone for fear of what could happen. Or we may try to control everything around us, obsessively monitoring every detail in an attempt to keep our lives safe and predictable. But while this strategy may help us to avoid short-term discomfort, it can also lead to a life of missed opportunities and regret.

Instead of letting fear rule your life, try to face it head-on. Identify the things that scare you and then find ways to confront them. Take small steps outside your comfort zone on a regular basis, and challenge yourself to try new things even when you're feeling anxious. It won't be easy, but it's worth it because the only way to truly live is to embrace the fear and learn to dance with it.

6. Getting too Attached to the Outcome of Setting a Boundary

When it comes to setting boundaries, one mistake that people often make is getting too attached to the outcome. In other words, they set a boundary with the expectation that the other person will react in a certain way. For example, they may set a boundary in an effort to get the other person to change their behavior. Or they may set a boundary in order to protect themselves from further hurt. While there's nothing wrong with wanting the other person to change their behavior or wanting to protect yourself, getting too attached to the outcome can actually backfire.

Here's why. When you're too attached to the outcome, you're more likely to be disappointed if things don't go the way you wanted. This can lead to resentment and even further conflict. Additionally, when you're too focused on the outcome, you may not be as present at the moment and may miss important cues from the other person.

It's important to remember that setting boundaries is about taking care of yourself and not about controlling the other person. Rather than getting too attached to the outcome, try to focus on being *present in the moment* and staying true to your own needs and values.

7. Being Too Subtle

When it comes to setting and enforcing boundaries, it's important to be clear and direct. After all, boundaries are all about communication. If you're too subtle, your message is likely to get lost in translation. For example, let's say you're not comfortable sharing your personal information with others. If you tell people that you're "not really a sharer," they may not understand that you're not interested in talking about certain topics. Instead, it's better to say something like, "I'm not comfortable sharing that information." That way, there's no confusion about your feelings on the matter. Or let's say you're trying to boundary-up in your romantic relationship by setting some standards for how you want to be treated. If you tell your partner that you don't want to be disrespected, they may interpret that to mean that they can still push your buttons as long as they apologize afterward. But if you say something like, "I need you to respect my wishes when it comes to X, Y, and Z," then there's no room for misinterpretation. In short, when it comes to setting boundaries, it's important to be as clear and direct as possible. Otherwise, you run the risk of having your boundaries crossed.

8. Overexplaining

When it comes to setting and maintaining personal boundaries, there is a fine line between being assertive and overexplaining oneself. For example, let's say you have a friend who is always asking you for favors. You may eventually start to feel used, and so you decide to set a boundary with this friend. From now on, you explain, you'll only do favors if they are reasonable and won't take up too much of your time.

Overexplaining is when someone feels the need to justify their personal boundaries to others, often in great detail. This can be harmful for a few different reasons. First, it can give others the impression that they are somehow entitled to an explanation as to why you have set a boundary. Secondly, it can make you seem defensive or uncertain about your own choices. Finally, it can open the door for others to try to talk you out of your boundaries. If you find yourself overexplaining your personal boundaries, try to remember that you are not obligated to justify your choices to anyone. You have a right to set boundaries as you see fit, and others will need to respect them whether they understand them or not.

9. Giving Up Easily

Setting and maintaining boundaries is vital to any healthy relationship – whether it be with a romantic partner, family member, friend, or even yourself. However, it can be easy to make mistakes when learning how to establish these boundaries. One such mistake is giving up too easily. This often happens when someone feels like they are constantly being pushed outside their comfort zone. They may start to feel like they are always the ones who have to make sacrifices and that their needs are never met. As a result, they may give up on setting boundaries altogether.

Of course, there will be times when it is necessary to compromise in order to maintain a healthy relationship. But it may be time to rethink your boundaries if you find yourself constantly giving in and never getting anything in return. Otherwise, you run the risk of ending up in a one-sided and emotionally draining relationship. So next time you're feeling like you're being pushed too far, take a step back and assess the situation. If you're not getting what you need from the relationship, it may be time to set new boundaries or walk away entirely.

10. Covering Too Many Boundaries

When it comes to setting and maintaining personal boundaries, there can be a lot of room for error. One common mistake is covering too much ground, so to speak. People try to protect themselves from any and all possible hurt, pain, or discomfort. This may sound like a good idea in theory, but in practice, it often leads to feeling isolated and cut off from the world. In other words, someone may try to set boundaries in every area of their life without taking into account their own needs and capabilities. Sticking to your own boundaries is essential in order to maintain a healthy sense of self. However, there is a fine line between maintaining your boundaries and becoming too rigid. This can lead to burnout, resentment, and a feeling of being trapped. Another possibility is that someone may set too many strict rules for themselves, preventing them from enjoying life and taking reasonable risks. Instead of rigidly adhering to their boundaries, it's important to be flexible and adaptable as needed. Ultimately, the goal should be to find a balance that meets your needs and those around you.

Instead of trying to protect yourself from everything, focus on setting up healthy boundaries that allow you to still experience life and maintain a sense of connection with others.

Tips To Rectify Self-Boundary Mistakes

We all have a tendency to try to do too much in an effort to feel better. We want to be good students, good employees, good friends, good spouses, and good parents. And we want to do it *all well*. So, we fill up our calendars and to-do lists, and we try to do everything that's expected of us. But eventually, we realize that we can't keep up the pace forever. Something has to give.

One of the best things you can do for yourself is to learn how to set boundaries. That means learning how to say "No" when you're already stretched too thin. It means learning to prioritize your commitments and focus on what's important to you. And it means learning how to let go of perfectionism and accepting that you can't do everything perfectly all the time.

1. **Make a list of your priorities.** What are the most important things in your life? Your family? Your health? Your job? Your hobbies? Figure out what's really important to you and make those things a priority.
2. **Be realistic** about what you can achieve in a day, a week, or even a month. You're not going to be able to do everything on your list, so figure out what's most important and focus on those things.
3. **Schedule some "me" time into your week.** You need time for yourself, even if it's just an hour or two. Use that time to relax, recharge, and connect with yourself.
4. **Learn to say "No" without feeling guilty.** It's okay to turn down invitations or requests for your time if you don't have the bandwidth for it. Just say no politely but firmly, and don't apologize for it.
5. **Let go of perfectionism.** You're not going to be able to do everything perfectly all the time, so stop beating yourself up over it. Learn to accept mistakes as part of the process and move on.
6. **Seek support from others** who understand what you're going through. There are likely other people in your life who are struggling with similar issues. Connect with them and lean on each other for support when needed.

Chapter 10: How to Make Your Boundaries 10x More Effective

Setting boundaries is critical for your mental health and for reaching your full potential. You must set the necessary boundaries to have strong self-esteem and build healthy relationships. You may find it challenging to set boundaries, particularly if you grew up in a household where boundaries were not respected. The good news is that you can always improve your ability to establish effective boundaries.

Establishing these boundaries means educating others on how to treat you, thereby protecting yourself from mistreatment. People sometimes treat you how they believe you want to be treated because you have yet to show them what you want. At other times, they treat you how you allow yourself to be treated.

Boundaries allow you to communicate your values. When you establish what you want, anyone who goes against it knows they are violating you. People will not accuse you of not knowing what you want because your boundaries have defined your priorities. We all require alone time to discover and grow, but you'll only be able to get this if you set boundaries.

Being yourself and doing things you find peaceful or comfortable is one way to live a happy and fulfilled life. You can enjoy your ideas, needs, thoughts, and feelings if you have healthy and effective boundaries. Boundaries allow you to be yourself rather than an extension of others or someone they coerced you into being. Your actions should result from your independent thoughts, not what others force you to do.

This chapter explains how you can increase the effectiveness of your boundaries tenfold. Even if you understand what boundaries are and have probably established some, it's important to remember that you can only reap its benefits if they are extremely effective. Ineffective boundaries are the same as no boundaries because they are constantly violated or crossed.

People can make you feel guilty for expressing your needs clearly, so be prepared for such outbursts. Humans are selfish by nature, as everyone wants their needs to be met whenever they want. As a result, expect your boundaries to irritate certain people who want to always have their own way with you. Boundaries benefit personal development, and no one should tell you otherwise. Knowing what boundaries are for will allow you to set them without feeling guilty.

Tips for How to Keep Your Boundaries up against All Resistance

Expect opposition from people who may be family, friends, or acquaintances. Dominating individuals will want to break all your boundaries to get their own way. It is also important to remember that everyone else has boundaries you must respect, even if they do not respect yours. It is sometimes easier to teach when you live by your own words.

When you set boundaries, be prepared to stick to them while also respecting the boundaries of others. When you want everyone to like and approve of you, keeping your boundaries becomes more difficult. You indirectly lower your boundaries when you choose the path of least resistance. You will find yourself repeatedly attempting to establish the same boundaries. Then it becomes clear that you must set your boundaries and adhere to them at all times, regardless of any opposition. The following are some pointers to help you keep your boundaries.

Recognize That You Can Be Wrong Rather Than Always Assuming You Are Correct

Your choices may make others uncomfortable, and you must be aware of this. Diplomatically communicate your needs. You may want to turn on the AC in extremely cold weather because it's your house and you're hot. Doing so could harm the health of anyone else in the house, which is wrong.

Forcing your needs on others will not help you succeed. Instead, be reasonable and willing to compromise if necessary. You can explain that you need the AC on because you are hot but that you'll turn it off in a few minutes if others cannot handle the cold. This action will clear your intentions without the need for a power struggle. Diplomacy can get you a lot of things that conflict cannot.

Be Direct about What You Want and Base Your Decisions on Yourself or Your Comfort

People can't argue with you about what's best for you, so it's easier to stick to your guns. When you make decisions about yourself, you automatically close the door to argument or resistance.

When Establishing or Enforcing Boundaries, Keep Them Concise and Clear

Have a natural limit, then remind yourself and the abuser calmly and without struggle about the consequences if the limit is crossed. Don't be aggressive in communicating your boundaries, don't explain too much, and don't force it. Instead, state them clearly and firmly. If you don't want your partner making sexual remarks about you in public, tell them, and don't feel bad about standing up for yourself.

You Can Control Your Actions but Not the Actions of Others

Consider what you want to do rather than what they want to do. When you realize that your actions will cause problems, figure out how to react to or resist those problems. You must plan ahead of time and present your boundary more acceptably.

Respect Yourself and Everything That Distinguishes You

Standing firm on your boundaries will require a lot of self-love. It will be difficult to tell others what you deserve and how you should be treated if you do not value yourself. Create a mindset that loves you and engages in activities that make you happy, such as dancing, exercising, or singing. When you fill your heart with beautiful things, it's difficult to let someone else treat you poorly.

Never Get Tired of Communicating Your Boundaries, Especially with Someone Who Disregards Them

It is necessary to state your boundaries but avoid making them constantly aggressive. For example, if your friend keeps calling your number until you pick up, you can say, "I understand you wanted to talk urgently, but it would be better to leave a message after a few calls, so I can respond as soon as I can." This action informed them of their error and clarified your preference.

Create a Framework to Help You Adapt to Your Limits

You may want some alone time every weekend. Set reminders and write them down to help you reinforce those boundaries. Try to stick to your time framework when work or family try to encroach on your space and consume every minute of your life. It will take some time, but don't lose sight of what truly matters.

Stay Consistent

Consistency will help you become acquainted with your rules while demonstrating to those watching that you are not playing games with your boundaries. When you relax your boundaries, those around you may become confused about what you truly desire. Once you've established your boundary, stick to it at all costs and punish those who cross it.

Establish Your Boundaries Early On

Establishing early boundaries enables people to adjust as they get to know you. It will be easier to maintain your boundaries if you set them out at the start of your relationship. Everyone will know where they stand, saving you frustration, resistance, confusion, and hurtful feelings.

Be Gentle With Everyone

This will allow you to change any boundaries that need to be adjusted. When you meet someone unfamiliar with your boundaries, or when you want to add more to the ones you already have, gradually introduce them. It will result in less resistance and more acceptance of your boundaries.

Take Some Time to Think about Why You Need to Set Boundaries

Understanding the benefits of maintaining your boundaries will encourage you to never give up in the face of opposition. It's fine to be in control of your psychology. It helps you comprehend what is happening around and within you. You can see a clearer picture of what you deserve if you think and reflect.

How to React When Someone Crosses or Insults Your Boundaries

Have you ever been in a situation where people repeatedly cross your boundaries? They act as if the limit does not exist, although you have spoken about it numerous times. Then they proceed to cross that line once more. Such situations can be very stressful. Boundaries will help you nurture healthy relationships, but overreacting when they are violated can ruin them. No matter how nice you are, some people will go out of their way to overstep your boundaries, perhaps to spite you or to get their own way. It would be best if you had a clear punishment for those who repeatedly violate your boundaries. Choose what is best for your wellbeing in any case. Consider the following:

Determine if You Can Negotiate the Boundaries

True, there are some people for whom you can make an exception, and adjusting your rules can help them respond positively to your boundaries. Having a flexible boundary that can be reshaped as needed is fine. Compromise should not include putting yourself in danger or under stress. Only change your boundaries to the extent necessary to protect your wellbeing. Don't do it because you feel obligated to or to please others.

Restate Your Boundaries as Often as Possible

Do this to allow for repentance. When dealing with people who cross your boundaries, you should be considerate. Their behavior could be a result of their boundary reinforcement. Set a limit or number of chances you can give someone before taking strict action.

Make Sure They Face the Consequences

Don't feel bad about making people face the consequences of their ill actions towards you. The results may be just what they need to start respecting your boundaries. If they do not change after that, be prepared to carry out the appropriate punishment.

Consider Separating Yourself

Separation protects your mental health and overall wellbeing. However, it isn't easy, especially if a family member or partner is involved. In situations like this, you can leave some communication with the person until you are ready. To make your reasons clear, gradually disconnect while reinforcing your boundaries. Healthy relationships respect boundaries, and you should not feel bad for leaving a relationship that does not respect yours. Disengagement occurs after several attempts at change have failed.

Standing Up for Yourself in a Conflict without Looking Like a Jerk

Situations requiring us to advocate for ourselves regularly arise, making it critical to learn how to be our hero. Conflict can arise from unexpected sources, but you must be prepared regardless. Different situations necessitate different strategies, but standing up for yourself can go a long way toward demonstrating how much you value yourself and others.

The atmosphere is already tense during the conflict, so you should articulate your actions well to avoid adding to the chaos. Standing up for yourself will earn you more respect from others. This act can help you believe in your worth and abilities.

To be able to advocate for yourself, you must have self-confidence. Make eye contact and stand up for what is best for you. It may be challenging to defend yourself if you are not assertive. However, with time and consistent practice, you'll be able to learn how to be your hero in times of conflict.

Standing up for yourself will undoubtedly boost your self-esteem. However, you should expect to be nervous when confronted with a conflicting situation. The following guides will assist you in defending yourself in the event of a conflict. Such experiences will teach valuable lessons, especially if you regularly protect yourself.

- When confronted with uncomfortable situations, saying "no" benefits your wellbeing. For example, if a colleague asks you to handle more work than you can reasonably do, explain why you are unable to accept and decline. Do not allow anyone to take your mental health lightly.
- In a stressful situation, present yourself so that your body language matches your words. Instead of mumbling or slouching, be confident and speak firmly/calmly. Maintain eye contact and maintain a straight posture.
- The boundaries you set may be the source of the conflict, prompting you to apologize out of guilt. Don't give in to that

feeling. Stick to your boundaries. There's nothing wrong with having needs and expecting others to respect them. When guilt overwhelms you, and you feel the need to apologize, explain your reasons briefly but skip the "I am sorry" part.

- Train and practice even before the conflict arises. Allow your imagination to run wild and create scenarios that could lead to conflict, then practice how to respond in such a situation. The more you practice, the easier it will be to speak confidently in public.
- Determine the imbalance that is causing conflict around you. People expect you to go above and beyond if you have previously done this for them. You'll be able to stand up for yourself without feeling bad once you've figured out what the source of the conflict is. Setting boundaries can help to prevent future conflict.
- When the environment becomes too toxic for you, leave without a fuss. Trying to have a conversation at that point may result in yelling and throwing hurtful words. Leave the room for fresh air and ensure you are not physically harmed. Don't be afraid to leave when it's the safest option in a chaotic situation.
- Don't be too quick to respond when someone says something to spite you or to make you overreact. Consider the situation, what prompted the person's words, and what the person expects you to do in response. You may see reasons to remain silent for the time being and respond much later. When the tension subsides, you can handle the situation much more effectively.
- You deserve respect and should not let anyone walk all over you. To boost your self-esteem, constantly remind yourself of your worth and values. Why, after all, do people not respect your boundaries? Why can't your coworkers, partners, family, and friends understand your requirements? There is no reason to be ashamed to ask for what you deserve.

Having Tough Conversations with Manipulators

Tough conversations are difficult because they are sensitive, but they are even more difficult to have with a manipulator. Manipulators always want to have their way, even if it means guilt-tripping you until you lose your resolve. Tough conversations easily trigger people and can lead to conflict and confrontation without achieving the conversation's goal.

How do you inform a colleague that they are misbehaving or performing poorly? How do you set boundaries and say "no" when the other person refuses? People get discouraged from trying due to fear. They would rather avoid the conversation than engage in it. No matter how bad you think a difficult conversation will be, it's better to have it now and deal with the short-term drama than to avoid it and face a bigger problem later.

Manipulators can be calm and reserved sometimes, but when you refuse all of their trials to force you to do their bidding, they unleash their aggressive side. This can come in the form of gaslighting, blackmail, and so on.

Setting boundaries around manipulators is difficult because doing so would deprive them of their power over you. But all is not lost. The points below can help you to navigate this difficult conversation without causing further harm.

- Maintain focus and calm by breathing as you speak. Keep your tone neutral. Take your time speaking because you could say something that doesn't express what you mean, leading to more misunderstanding.
- Pay attention as they express themselves. You may find evidence that allows you to stand firm or impose necessary consequences.
- Deliver your message calmly and quickly, then exit the conversation as soon as possible. Staying longer allows the manipulator to mess with your mind. Don't let it happen!
- They will use emotional arguments to persuade or distract you but do not give in.
- Don't try to silence them because doing so may expose you to their manipulations. Listen to them, and if you can't do what they want you to do, refer them to someone who can.
- Maintain eye contact and confidence. Being shy will not protect you from their manipulative tactics, so demonstrate your bravery and confidence.

How to Extend Your Boundaries into Social Media and an Online Environment

Social media is a no man's land where people infringe on the privacy of others without their knowledge. There's a lot of self-interest flying around, and some people want to abuse and use you.

How important is the online/social media space to you, and how much can you handle without jeopardizing your mental health? Are you constantly glued to your phone?

Without a doubt, social media has positive aspects, but without boundaries, you wouldn't know when to stop. Boundaries help you to protect your sanity and engage in online environments only to maximize your productivity rather than wasting your day and night online aimlessly. Follow the guidelines below to set your online boundaries.

Be Picky about Who You Follow and Who You Friend

Posts that do not contribute to your growth and happiness are not intended to appear on your wall. Remove all contact with toxic people. Follow accounts that are beneficial to you with caution and without remorse. Continue cleaning until you achieve peace in your social media account. The quality of your friends is more important than the quantity.

Configure Your Account to Vet Friend Invitations/Requests

You should choose who you want to be friends with online, just as offline. Examine the account of the person who wants to be your friend to see if their content will benefit you in any way.

Identify Your Goal with Social Media

Do you want to network for business or to pass the time? Make a schedule for yourself and make sure you meet your daily goals. Your response will influence which friends and content you should entertain and consume.

Avoid Dragging and Insulting Comments

You should protect yourself from negativity online, so ignore or block those who post offensive or violent content.

Spend Less Time Online

Deactivate your social media account notifications and spend less time online. If you're online for fun and business, make a separate schedule for each and stick to it. It would be best if you devoted your energy to more important aspects of your life, such as your close relationships, family, and health.

Value Family Time More

When you're not using social media, mute your phone so it doesn't interfere with your other activities. Staying away from your phone at home will teach your children the value of family time.

Don't Be Too Quick to Trust Online Friends

If you find a stranger interesting online, wait to reveal too much about yourself quickly. When you rush to give a stranger personal information, they may use it against you in the future. Remember that what bad people show online is a facade to make a good first impression. Keep an eye out for inconsistencies that reveal who they truly are.

To find out if the people in your life or around you are manipulative, keep a journal of your interactions with them and think about it when you're settled.

_____

_____

_____

How did you react to a recent negative action?

_____

_____

_____

What are the mistakes you've made in expressing your boundaries, and what would you do differently now?

_____

_____

_____

Do you consider a boundary a solid wall separating you from other people? There are no visible boundaries, but clear emotions can be expressed for a healthier life and relationships. Boundaries are ways to communicate to others what you deserve or require and how you should be treated. With boundaries, you'll take better care of yourself. As a result, you must master the act of setting effective boundaries. Setting boundaries without enforcing or maintaining them will bear little fruit.

Feeling bad about showing others what makes you happy, comfortable, and productive is pointless. When people cross your boundary, don't be too hard on yourself because they may simply be trying to meet their needs. You can make your boundaries flexible to accommodate others or rigid to keep them away.

Whatever boundaries you choose, stick to what you find comfortable. When you create an exception to meet another person's needs, make it clear that you are doing so for a reason. It will notify them that you may not extend such a favor again—the more effective your boundaries, the better the outcome and success.

Conclusion

Setting boundaries is the best way to tell others how to treat you. The boundaries you set lead to your growth and help you achieve so much in life. To avoid the drama and chaos associated with boundary resistance, it is preferable to establish and communicate your boundaries from the onset of a relationship.

The consistent times you eat, report to work, and enjoy alone time are all due to the boundaries you set. Others may not agree with your boundaries, but remember that it is about your wellbeing, not theirs. Always seeking to please others will rob you of your happiness. Therefore, you should become accustomed to saying "No" when necessary.

People will remember you for the one time you turned them down, even though you could have satisfied them a million times. Why subject yourself to such mental torment? Be resolute in communicating your desires without guilt, and others will accept your stance.

This book showed you how to avoid guilt and set healthy boundaries. The guides are written in plain language to facilitate comprehension and application. You may feel insecure about many things, but in the preceding chapters, you'll have learned how to transform that insecurity into confidence.

Insecurity can indicate low self-esteem, which makes you susceptible to boundary violations and manipulation. Your relationship will not suffer if you learn how to avoid the errors that can destroy it. Growth is a continuous process; you are meant to continue learning and implementing things that will make your life easier and more enjoyable.

Parenting is difficult, but we've given you tools to deal with challenging relatives and improve your child's behavior. Some family members may want you to do their bidding even if it puts you out of your comfort zone. They'll find someone else to leech on if you break down. Losing yourself to please others is similar to providing a temporary solution to a long-term issue.

Do you have friends who only see the negative side of everything and everyone? With such friends, you shouldn't always attempt to prove a point. Sometimes you should avoid arguing with them to avoid mental stress, but if the toxicity becomes intolerable, you may want to consider detaching yourself from them.

Negativity is bad for your mental health, and you should avoid surrounding yourself with it. Too many toxic individuals in the world wish to dampen your spirit with their negativity, but you must resist them.

A commanding boss may expect you to continue doing whatever they ask of you. You'll lose your freedom if you do their bidding. Instead of trying to please everyone to receive favors, you can be cheerful at work, genuinely care about your coworkers, and only accept workloads you can effectively manage.

Allow the promotion to come to you because you qualified for it in terms of potential and efficiency rather than as a form of compensation. When you qualify for a promotion, the company does not want to lose you. Don't try to fake your personality or take on too many tasks in the hope of making everyone like you. Only those who can relate to your true values and norms will like you.

Genuine encounters and experiences breed true relationships. Keep it real at all times, and you'll attract genuine friends. Finally, boundaries allow you to be yourself, and you should never give up on ensuring that they are highly effective.

Here's another book by Andy Gardner that you might like

Free Bonus from Andy Gardner

Hi!

My name is Andy Gardner, and first off, I want to THANK YOU for reading my book.

Now you have a chance to join my exclusive email list related to human psychology and self-development so you can get the ebook below for free as well as the potential to get more ebooks for free! Simply click the link below to join.

P.S. Remember that it's 100% free to join the list.

Access your free bonuses here:
https://livetolearn.lpages.co/andy-gardner-how-to-set-boundaries-paperback/

References

Charlie. (2020, June 17). 5 tips to maintain healthy boundaries (and not feel guilty). Www.yourtimetogrow.com. https://www.yourtimetogrow.com/5-tips-to-maintain-healthy-boundaries-and-not-feel-guilty/

Boundaries: What are they, and how to create them. (n.d.). Uic.edu. https://wellnesscenter.uic.edu/news-stories/boundaries-what-are-they-and-how-to-create-them/

Brady, K. (2019, June 5). 5 types of boundaries for your relationship. Keir Brady Counseling Services. https://keirbradycounseling.com/relationship-boundaries/

Ferguson, P. L. (n.d.). Boundaries as a recovery concept by. Peggyferguson.com. http://www.peggyferguson.com/userfiles/10846/file/articlespdf/Boundaries%20as%20a%20Recovery%20Concept.pdf

Hazelden Publishing. (1989). Setting Boundaries. HarperCollins.

Healthy vs. Unhealthy boundaries. (n.d.). Healthyrelationshipsinitiative.org. https://healthyrelationshipsinitiative.org/healthy-vs-unhealthy-boundaries/

Menachem, S. (2022, August 10). Healthy vs. Unhealthy boundaries. Menachem Psychotherapy Group. https://menachempsychotherapygroup.com/healthy-vs-unhealthy-boundaries/

Morin, M. (2021, November 12). How to Set Boundaries and Not Feel Guilty (Five-Step Plan to Create Boundaries). Morin Holistic Therapy. https://morinholistictherapy.com/how-to-set-boundaries-and-not-feel-guilty-five-step-plan-to-create-boundaries/

Assertiveness. (n.d.). Psychology Today. https://www.psychologytoday.com/us/basics/assertiveness

Being assertive: Reduce stress, communicate better. (2022, May 13). Mayo Clinic. https://www.mayoclinic.org/healthy-lifestyle/stress-management/in-depth/assertive/art-20044644

Brigham, T. (2022, February 4). 5 psychological tricks that will make you look and feel more confident, according to a psychotherapist. CNBC. https://www.cnbc.com/2022/02/04/psychological-tricks-that-will-make-you-look-and-feel-more-confident-in-front-of-others.html

Brigham, T. (2022, February 4). 5 psychological tricks that will make you look and feel more confident, according to a psychotherapist. CNBC. https://www.cnbc.com/2022/02/04/psychological-tricks-that-will-make-you-look-and-feel-more-confident-in-front-of-others.html

Guide to good posture. (2017). Bones, Joints and Muscles. https://medlineplus.gov/guidetogoodposture.html

7 tips for handling conflict in your relationship. (2016, November 4). One Love Foundation. https://www.joinonelove.org/learn/handling_conflict/

Barrie, Z. (2016, August 10). 5 signs you're dating someone who is trying to change you. Elite Daily. https://www.elitedaily.com/dating/signs-dating-someone-change-you/1578738

Beck, M. (2011, December 6). A fair fight: Healthy conflict creates healthy boundaries. Martha Beck. https://marthabeck.com/2011/12/a-fair-fight-healthy-conflict-creates-healthy-boundaries/

Chatel, A. (2016, June 15). How to deal with A partner who can't handle conflict. Bustle. https://www.bustle.com/articles/166961-how-to-deal-with-a-partner-who-cant-handle-conflict

How to set boundaries with family. (n.d.). Psychology Today. https://www.psychologytoday.com/us/blog/pain-explained/201912/how-set-boundaries-family

Radin, S. (2019, November 13). How to create boundaries with toxic family members. Allure. https://www.allure.com/story/toxic-family-how-create-boundaries

Simperingham, G. (2013, April 29). The importance of healthy boundaries in the family. The Way of the Peaceful Parent. https://www.peacefulparent.com/can-you-maintain-and-model-healthy-boundaries/

Pincus, D., & Lmhc, M. S. (2013, May 14). How to set healthy boundaries with your child. Empowering Parents. https://www.empoweringparents.com/article/parental-roles-how-to-set-healthy-boundaries-with-your-child/

Simperingham, G. (2013, April 29). The importance of healthy boundaries in the family. The Way of the Peaceful Parent.

https://www.peacefulparent.com/can-you-maintain-and-model-healthy-boundaries/

Encouraging good behaviour: 15 tips. (2020, September 24). Raising Children Network. https://raisingchildren.net.au/toddlers/behaviour/encouraging-good-behaviour/good-behaviour-tips

Bansal, V. (2021, November 11). How to deal with negative people without going crazy. TechTello. https://www.techtello.com/how-to-deal-with-negative-people/

Beard, C. (2019, June 26). How to deal with negative people. The Blissful Mind. https://theblissfulmind.com/how-to-deal-with-negative-people/

Chua, C. (2010a, June 28). 9 ways to manage people who bother you. Lifehack. https://www.lifehack.org/articles/communication/9-ways-to-manage-people-who-bother-you.html

Chua, C. (2010b, August 9). 9 helpful tips to deal with negative people. Lifehack. https://www.lifehack.org/articles/communication/9-helpful-tips-to-deal-with-negative-people.html

Edelstein, A. (2022, September 21). How to deal with a negative friend —. Austin Therapy and EMDR. https://www.austintherapyemdr.com/blog/how-to-handle-negative-friend-partner

10 signs you're a chronic people pleaser—and how to stop. (n.d.). Career Contessa. https://www.careercontessa.com/advice/people-pleaser/

Castrillon, C. (2022, July 6). 10 ways to stop being A people pleaser at work. Forbes. https://www.forbes.com/sites/carolinecastrillon/2022/07/06/10-ways-to-stop-being-a-people-pleaser-at-work/?sh=728d770d2c36

Hlatswayobusisiwe, P. by. (2021, August 18). Are you a people pleaser? 5 reasons why you are not getting promoted. Black Women in the Workplace. https://blackwomenintheworkplace.com/2021/08/18/are-you-a-people-pleaser-5-reasons-why-you-are-not-getting-promoted/

Raypole, C. (2019, December 5). People pleaser: 22 signs and tips. Healthline. https://www.healthline.com/health/people-pleaser

Shethna, J. (2016, July 15). Why being a people-pleaser is bad for professional life? EDUCBA. https://www.educba.com/ways-you-can-stop-being-a-people-pleaser/

Elizabeth Earnshaw, L. (2020, January 2). I'm A therapist & here are 6 things people get wrong about boundaries. Mindbodygreen. https://www.mindbodygreen.com/articles/common-mistakes-people-make-when-setting-boundaries

Hailey, L. (2022, April 15). How to set boundaries: 5 ways to draw the line politely. Science of People. https://www.scienceofpeople.com/how-to-set-boundaries/

Lee, C. I. (2022, June 12). 10 common mistakes when setting personal boundaries. LA Concierge Psychologist. https://laconciergepsychologist.com/blog/mistakes-setting-personal-boundaries/

Martin, S. (2022, September 9). 5 boundary mistakes. Live Well with Sharon Martin. https://www.livewellwithsharonmartin.com/boundary-mistakes/

What are Personal Boundaries? (n.d.). Berkeley.edu. https://uhs.berkeley.edu/sites/default/files/relationships_personal_boundaries.pdf

Martin, S. (2019, June 18). 5 tips that make setting boundaries easier. Live Well with Sharon Martin. https://www.livewellwithsharonmartin.com/tips-for-setting-boundaries/

Pattemore, C. (2021, June 3). 10 ways to build and preserve better boundaries. Psych Central. https://psychcentral.com/lib/10-way-to-build-and-preserve-better-boundaries

Neda Brasanac, M. (2022, June 6). What to do when someone crosses your boundaries (again). Real Life Counselling. https://www.reallifecounselling.com/2022/06/what-to-do-when-someone-crosses-your-boundaries-again/

Eatough, E. (n.d.). How to stand up for yourself: 8 ways to make it work. Betterup.com. https://www.betterup.com/blog/how-to-stand-up-for-yourself

Stebbins, P. (2016, April 8). Difficult conversations: Aggression, manipulation & emotion. Linkedin.com. https://www.linkedin.com/pulse/difficult-conversations-aggression-manipulation-emotion-stebbins

(N.d.). Lovegrowbehappy.com. https://www.lovegrowbehappy.com/boundaries-on-social-media

www.ingramcontent.com/pod-product-compliance
Lightning Source LLC
Chambersburg PA
CBHW070337010526
44107CB00004B/531